D0913297

Without A Friend

...why the world is turning against Israel
and the Jewish people

A Jewish Perspective

By

R. Baruch Ph.D.

Copyright © 2012 by R. Baruch, Ph.D.

ISBN 978-0-7414-7271-7 Paperback
ISBN 978-0-7414-7272-4 eBook

Printed in the United States of America

Published January 2013

INFINITY PUBLISHING
1094 New DeHaven Street, Suite 100
West Conshohocken, PA 19428-2713
Toll-free (877) BUY BOOK
Local Phone (610) 941-9999
Fax (610) 941-9959
Info@buybooksontheweb.com
www.buybooksontheweb.com

Table of Contents

Foreword

The purpose of this book is to present the Biblical view of the end times as revealed in the writings of both the Old and New Testaments. What makes this work unique is that texts which are sacred to Judaism are also consulted in order to provide a greater understanding of the intent of the various authors of the Biblical books. Insights from rabbinical scholars are also considered and offer a wider perspective than most works from a believing standpoint. It must be noted that these extra Biblical writings, as well as the rabbinical interpretations, should **not** be viewed as authoritative or possessing inspiration, but simply useful in providing background as framework for a greater comprehension of the original intent of the Biblical revelation.

This book will provide the reader with numerous reasons why **Replacement Theology**, the view that the Church replaces Israel and therefore none of the Biblical promises concerning Israel and the Jewish people should be expected to be fulfilled, is scripturally invalid and should be rejected. It clearly shows why there should be a strong expectation for the Jewish people to return to their historical homeland and the world to turn against the modern State of Israel.

All scriptural citations are the work of the author as he translated them from the original language, considering the textual variants. The insight of numerous years of study in rabbinical centers provided valuable insight in arriving at a vantage point that most believers in Yeshua (Jesus) of Nazareth do not possess. The intent of this book is not to provide the reader with a textbook approach to the major thoughts and authors on the subject of the end times; rather this book is an inductive study of Scripture from a Jewish perspective. Special effort was taken in order to ensure the readability of this book for all individuals. Although concise, this book offers a thorough handling of the major events and primary texts that address the last days.

Finally, the intended audience for this book is not only those who come from the Christian faith, but also Jewish individuals, who will find how Israel should be understood and her role in the end times most enlightening. Even those individuals who have no personal attachment to a religious tradition will be forced to agree that much of what the Bible foretells for the last days seems to be drawing near especially in light of the growth of Islam. This book is certainly not an attempt to please all; quite the contrary, it challenges many of the accepted views of eschatology by Evangelicals by offering a Scriptural presentation that is rooted in a methodology that is thoroughly hermeneutically sound.

Chapter 1

"The Call for Change"

Even though many people throughout the world may define themselves as religious, few base their religious perspectives on sacred texts. Most simply identify with a major religion and adapt a few of its major doctrines to suit their views. In other words, many individuals like identifying themselves as part of some religious movement, but are not well versed in this religion, nor are they highly committed to it. Often one's religious identification is rooted in cultural factors rather than strong personal convictions based in theological beliefs. When considering Christianity and its various views concerning the end times, it is safe to say that most people who identify themselves as Christian are incapable of presenting a Biblically-based view for what Scripture attests will take place in the last days.

Failure to know the truth concerning the end times will cause one, Christian or not, to be unprepared for what is going to take place in the last days and most likely be deceived by the enemy. When looking at the general population, the prevailing view is that G-d is not so involved in one's life or the world which He created. When confronted with some of the catastrophic events that Scripture reveals will take place in the future, most individuals likely will respond in a very similar manner to what one reads in the third chapter of Second Peter,

"Knowing this first, that shall come in the last days in mockery, mockers, in their own desire walking (i.e. conducting their lives). *And saying, 'where is the promise of His* (i.e. the Messiah's) *coming?' For since the fathers have fallen asleep* (i.e. have died); *all in the same way continues as from the beginning of creation."* 2 Peter 3:3-4

1

This text reveals that a great number of people will scoff at the idea that there is something unique about any period of time, let alone believe that this world as we know it will come to an end. Hence most will be totally unprepared for what Yeshua said concerning the events of the end times, "For (these things) *must take place,*"(Matthew 24:6). Therefore there is an absolute must for the prophesied events to come about.

Another key aspect of the aforementioned text from Second Peter is that people will be guided and influenced by their sinful desires. Such desires blind people spiritually; hence individuals will not be able to discern the significance of what is occurring at this time or how these events relate to G-d's plan for the last days. Because most of the events of this period are related to harsh tribulation, eventually all will have to acknowledge that some kind of change is necessary. Perhaps initially these trials will be viewed as nothing more than catastrophes similar to other disasters that have happened before; but due to their intensity and frequency, most will arrive at the conclusion that some kind of dramatic action is needed.

Before outlining what this action will be, it is necessary to understand what things will take place which signal that the end times are upon us. Both Biblical and rabbinical sources speak to a similar description. First of all, one must remember that the end times will give rise to the Coming (Return) of the Messiah. In the Talmud, Tractate Sanhedrin 98a, Rabbi Yehuda says the Messiah will come in the generation that is full of licentiousness. He also says that those who fear sin will be despised, and truth will be absent. Rabbi Yehuda concludes by evaluating those who identify themselves as followers of the G-d of Israel and states that heresy will be prevalent among them. The Apostle Paul speaks of similar conditions when he writes that a great apostasy will take place in the last days prior to the coming of Messiah (See Second Thessalonians 2:3). Not only will there be moral and spiritual decline leading up to the end times, but Scripture reveals that there will be three sources of unrest. These three sources are political, environmental, and economical.

Political Turmoil

Yeshua taught on the Mt. of Olives, a place of great eschatological significance,

"And you shall hear of wars and rumors of wars, see that you are not troubled; because these must happen, but it is not yet the end. For ethnic groups will rise up against ethnic groups and nation against nation..." Matthew 24:6-7

This text teaches that in the last days there will be political unrest. One of the causes of such unrest will be an increase in the number of wars. Not only will there be wars taking place in numerous places, but there will also be the threat of additional wars breaking out, giving great concern to all. It is most significant that one pays attention to the actual words which the text uses. Whereas most translations state *"nations will rise up against nations"*, the actual word which is employed is the Greek word *"ethnos"* from where the English word "ethnic" is derived. Therefore an important sign concerning the end times is that there will be conflicts between different ethnic groups.

At the time of the writing of this book, there are numerous conflicts of this type taking place in Africa and the Middle East, which are not based in national boundaries, but what is commonly referred to as "tribal conflicts". The basis for these conflicts often goes back many generations and it is most difficult to find a resolution. Due to the fact that these are not "formal" wars and those who fight are not typical soldiers representing a recognized army, these conflicts often involve entire villages being wiped out. Women and children are targets as one ethnic group attempts to exterminate another. Because of the barbaric nature of such disputes, international bodies usually get involved, attempting to establish peace. These types of "peace keeping" efforts are extremely costly and usually do not bring a lasting stability to the region. Currently, such conflicts are occurring in Pakistan, Darfur, Russia, and Iraq just to name a few.

Along with these ethnic conflicts, Yeshua also spoke about the more traditional type of wars between nation states. In the Matthew 24 text the word "kingdom" is used, but certainly our concept of a nation would also apply. Regardless of which type of war is actually occurring, these conflicts have a destabilizing effect in the region. This destabilization is the basis for a call for change. Some have pointed out that due to the numerous conflicts that are taking place in the world, and the inability of the nation(s) in which they are happening to deal with such conflicts effectively, world organizations must be utilized. Hence, many see these conflicts, especially those rooted in ethnic factors, as a justification for globalization. Although globalization will be discussed later in our study, it is sufficient to state at this time that globalization is a major part of the Antichrist's plan to gain control over the world.

Environmental Turmoil

The cost of natural disasters, both financial and to human life, are often considerable. One only needs to mention the earthquake in Haiti in 2010 and the one off the coast of Japan in 2011 and the tsunami which followed to be convinced of this. Yeshua in the same passage from Matthew 24 also said,

> "...and there shall be famines and earthquakes at (various) places. But all these things are the beginning of sorrows."
>
> Matthew 24:7-8

Before we discuss the implications of famines and earthquakes, let us focus on the latter portion of the citation— "*But all these things are the beginning of sorrows.*" The intent of this statement is to inform the reader that the sources of turmoil that will occur in the end times are simply the preparation for the major events of this period of time. Because the world will suffer an inordinate number of famines and earthquakes, desperate times will present themselves. The two primary causes of famine are poor weather conditions (usually droughts) and pestilence. The spread of diseases is also a frequent outcome of famines and earthquakes. It is important that one notices that Messiah placed the political unrest and wars along side of the famines and earthquakes, thereby revealing a situation of great misery and instability.

More and more, when a country faces a natural disaster or some other severe event, the world community is called upon to offer assistance. Today such world agencies are being stretched very thin. Imagine what will happen when the events that Yeshua spoke of begin to become a reality. The result will be that they collapse under the numerous requests for assistance and will not be able to respond in any meaningful way. It will become very clear that a change will be required to handle these desperate times.

Economic Turmoil

One does not need to hold a doctorate in economics and finance to understand that the political and environmental turmoil that the Scripture foretells as the preparation for the last days will bring about poor economic conditions. At the time of this writing (Summer 2011) much of the world is suffering an economic down turn. The chief economic powerhouse, the United States of America, is 14 trillion dollars in debt and this figure does not include the trillions of additional dollars of underfunded programs which the U.S. government is obligated to pay. Countries such as Greece, Spain, Portugal, and Italy are also severely in debt. Along with the American fiscal decline is a decline in respect for American foreign policy. In short, America can suggest its desires to other nations, but the days when it could all but impose its policies upon other nations are long gone.

With America's leadership capacity greatly weakened, it is an encouragement to tyrants to flaunt their power and commit acts of atrocities against others. One only needs to look back to the period of the Second World War to realize that without America's involvement, Hitler's Third Reich would have successfully gained control of Europe, Northern Africa, and parts of Asia. The world would have looked very different today had there not been a strong America. Simply stated, an American decline in power will bring about swift changes in the world, and these changes will be most negative.

Turmoil and the Book of Revelation

Thus far we have only touched briefly on these three sources of turmoil that will bring about severe hardship throughout the world and thereby bring a mass call for change. In order to provide greater understanding of these times, we will now look to a passage from the book of Revelation for insight.

In the sixth chapter of Revelation six seals are listed. In this section only the first four seals will be discussed. In the previous chapter of Revelation, a book is seen in the right hand of the One Who sits upon the heavenly throne. This book has seven seals, which may be understood as chapters. The point which must be understood is that the seals are closed and no one, except Messiah Himself, is worthy to open them. This fact informs the reader that in spite of the chaos that will accompany the last days, it is Messiah Who is in charge. In other words, nothing is going to happen that Yeshua does not allow, both the event itself and the timing of each event. Even though He is in charge, one should not conclude that Messiah is the cause of all of these things. G-d is sovereign and omniscient; yet, simply because He knows all that would take place from eternity past does not mean that He has caused all things to happen.

The seals do not only represent chapters, but also stages for these various events which are prophesied. Now we shall begin our examination of the first four seals. When the Lamb, a reference to the crucified Messiah, Who now resides in the heavens, opens the first seal, thunder is heard. Obviously thunder is a loud noise and captures the attention of those who hear it. Hence, this section opens up with a call to the reader to pay special attention to the revelation contained in the seals. John, who is the one receiving the vision, is summoned to come closer and look (Revelation 6:1). As he looks, he sees one sitting on a white horse holding a bow. Many have interpreted this one to be the Messiah; however further study of the following verses will clearly reveal that this one is not the same One Who is mentioned upon a white horse in Revelation 19:11,

"And I saw the heaven being opened, and behold, a white horse and One sitting upon it, called Faithful and True, and in righteousness He judges and makes war."

This One is indeed Messiah Yeshua; however the one which is seen in the first seal of Revelation chapter six is an imposter. He rides upon a white horse professing to be a man of peace, but time will disclose the truth—that he is a mass killer. In the second verse of chapter six the reader is informed that he was given a crown and he goes about and conquers. Earlier in this verse it is said that he holds a bow, a weapon symbolizing power. What one should glean from this verse is that a ruler will emerge possessing great power and he will conquer many nations and will present himself as a man of justice, loving peace. This is the first stage of the preparation for the last days.

When the second seal is opened another horse is seen; however this horse is red. This informs the reader that the peace which was promised by this new leader was very short lived. For the text reads,

"And another horse came out, red; and the one who sat upon him, it was given to this one to take peace from the earth, and in order to slay one another, it also was given to him a great sword." Revelation 6:4

It is not surprising that this horse is red, as red is the color of blood. It is also significant that another weapon of war is mentioned, this time a sword instead of a bow. The point that one should not fail to notice is that what is revealed in these first two seals is most similar to Yeshua's statement that there will be

7

wars and rumors of wars. Not only did Messiah mention wars, but famines and pestilence as well. Therefore, if there is indeed a correlation between Matthew 24 and Revelation 6, one should expect that famines and pestilence should also be mentioned in the seals.

In the third seal a black horse is seen and the one who sat upon it had a pair of balances in his hand. Obviously the purpose of the balances was to weigh things in order to determine their value. In the next verse one reads,

> *"And I heard a voice in the midst of the four beasts saying, a measure of wheat for a denarius and three measures of barley for a denarius..."* Revelation 6:6a

Although some translations render the Greek word denarius as a "penny", such a translation fails to convey the intent of the Scriptural verse. A denarius is a common man's daily wage. The measure that is referred to in this verse is equal to the amount that a typical person would consume in a day, in other words a very small amount for an entire day's wage. The message of the text is that food prices are going to soar. When do food prices rise at the staggering rate as this text reveals? The answer is in times of famine. The color of the horse being black may also symbolize death, as one of the worst plagues known to human history was called the black plague.

Once again the situation described in this section of the book of Revelation is that of great suffering and hardship. Death is prevalent and the text seems to imply that most of the world is affected by these happenings. It is at the end of this section dealing with the third seal that a particular sentence appears,

> *"...And the oil and the wine, you shall not harm."*
> Revelation 6:6b

It would be most unusual that food prices would rise to unbelievable heights, but the price for oil and wine would not be at all affected. It is for this reason many scholars understand this statement in an allegorical manner. Many times in the Bible oil is used in regard to the Holy Spirit.

"And Samuel took the horn of oil and he anointed him (David) in the midst of his brothers and the Spirit of the L-rd prospered David from that day on..." I Samuel 16:13

When one was anointed with oil, the Spirit of G-d would come upon that individual. Wine is used in the rabbinical writings to convey joy and gladness. Also in the book of Psalms there is a reference to this same usage,

"And wine will gladden a man's heart..." Psalm 104:15

The intent of the verse is that in spite of all the trials and hardships that will characterize this period, the Holy Spirit will still continue to minister in the life of believers and because our joy is rooted in our relationship with the living G-d, the misery will not in any way diminish our joy in Yeshua.

It is the fourth seal which is most informative for one being able to understand the origin of these trials. When the fourth seal is opened another horse is seen, this time the color is not so easy to discern. The Greek word which is used is related to the color green. Once again knowledge of Jewish religious texts proves to be helpful. Whereas the color blue relates to the heavens, green symbolizes this world. Hence the one who is riding upon this horse is not related to the heavenly realm, but he is of this world. In fact, this is related to the one who Yeshua called the prince of this world (John 12:31). It was in this vein that Yeshua warned individuals about being too attached to this world and following in its ways, rather than having one's beliefs and philosophies rooted in scriptural truth. He said that His Kingdom was not of this world (John 18:36). Paul continues this same idea and admonishes believers not to be conformed to the world (Romans 12:2).

Therefore it is also quite clear that this one is obviously not of the same purpose as the Messiah. This one is also identified with the

R. Baruch, Ph.D.

name "Death", while Yeshua is identified with life! Furthermore the reader is told that hell followed with him (Revelation 6:8). The chief hermeneutical aid in arriving at the proper interpretation of these verses is found in the latter half of this verse.

"And it was given to them authority over a fourth of the earth to kill with a sword, with famine, and with death and by the beasts of the earth."

It is most significant that contained in the forth seal there is a summary of the first three seals. The purpose for this is to show that there is a correlation between all four seals. Also notice that in the first seal the one who sits on the white horse goes forth to conquer. In the summary statement the reader is told that he had authority over a fourth of the earth, i.e. that he conquered a fourth of the earth. In regard to the second seal, verse four mentions he has a sword. So, too, in the summary statement is a sword mentioned. It needs to be pointed out that two different words are used. In the fourth verse the word translated "sword" refers to the type of sword of an executioner; whereas in the eighth verse a broader sword is mentioned that is more frightful. The purpose for the change is to reveal to the reader that the killings were not only to dispose of those who oppose this leader, but also to intimidate others from resisting him in the future. The summary statement also mentions that people will die by means of famine, identical to the third seal. Also included in verse eight is the word "death", which links the first three seals with the fourth as the one who sat on the fourth horse is called "Death". In order to show the dire conditions of this time, it is revealed that wild animals will enter into cities and attack individuals, killing them. Most scholars attribute this to the severe lack of food available in the land.

Once again the purpose of this summary statement is to teach the reader that there is a commonality to the first four seals. This being the case, each of the first three riders is connected to the one called "Death". Their origin is hell also. Therefore the point that must be grasped from this passage from Revelation chapter six is that the initial period of hardships and suffering is Satanic in nature. This point will prove to be vital in comprehending much of what will take place in the last days. This fact is also necessary in assisting one in arriving at a proper understanding of the L-rd's promises to believers for this period of time.

It is now clear from just a few texts that the end times are indeed troublesome times. Individuals will be willing to turn to almost anyone who offers assistance. As has been previously stated, the various world agencies will prove to be incapable of handling the numerous natural disasters, let alone the political and economic instability.

Instability: Catalyst for Change

One of the basic principles that has been seen throughout history is that when there is stability in a government, change comes very slowly; however at times of great peril and instability, dramatic changes come swiftly. The populace in such times of uncertainty and suffering will demand someone do something. The old adage, "Desperate times call for desperate action" will ring true. It is at periods such as these that one who could never ascend to political leadership under normal circumstances will take control. Probably the best example of this occurred in Germany in the 1930's. Hindsight makes it very clear that Adolf Hitler was exactly what Germany did not need, but nevertheless his rhetoric proved to be just what the masses wanted to hear during this period of Germany's instability.

What must be understood is that during difficult times Germany chose one who was blatantly against the principles of Scripture, rather than turning to G-d and relying upon Him and His word to lead Germany to a righteous solution. So, too, in the last days, history will repeat itself, as a man of lawlessness will gain control over the world.

11

Chapter 2

"Israel: The World Leader"

Israel today does not have many allies. Her traditional "best friend", the United States of America, has distanced herself from the only democracy in the Mideast. This shift away from Israel began during the elder George Bush's presidency. Under the leadership of James Baker, a "peace plan", which called for two states west of the Jordan River, began to gather support. Presidents Clinton, Bush 2, and Obama simply have moved the ball forward to where most diplomats see it only as a matter of time before a Palestinian State emerges. How a Palestinian State figures into G-d's prophetic plan shall be discussed in detail later on in our discussion. The focus of this chapter is Israel as a divine source of deliverance.

Any good student of the Bible knows that patterns can be seen repeating themselves in the Scriptures. One such pattern occurs in the book of Genesis. During the days of Joseph, it was prophesied that seven years of prosperity would be followed by seven years of intense famine. It was Joseph, the son of Jacob (Israel), who proved to be a "savior" for the world. In other words, had not Joseph risen to power, the world would have been totally unprepared for the period of trials that it was about to enter. The point is this: G-d provided a leader and equipped him with the wisdom and the knowledge to guide the people through this time of peril. However in the last days, similar to the period of World War II, much of the world will choose a leader who will bring travesty instead of deliverance.

Why is Israel Important?

Early in the book of Genesis man fell out of favor with G-d due to sin. Because of sin, man became in need of redemption. The account of Noah demonstrates an important Biblical truth. In this section G-d chooses Noah, who is called a righteous and blameless man who walked with G-d (Genesis 6:9). Because the earth was full of violence and immorality, the L-rd decided to destroy all people and begin humanity again, this time with Noah and his family. Rabbinical interpreters understand this as a type of an experiment for the sake of the reader. In other words, G-d of course knew what the outcome would be; however He played it out for the benefit of the reader of the Bible so he would learn a vital truth. In essence, G-d took the best man and filled the world once more with his descendants. The question that this experiment would answer is: would the world be in a different spiritual condition because of Noah? Earlier on in chapter six of the book of Genesis, the reader is told that G-d regretted that He had made man, in light of how man's actions corrupted the state of the earth. Now, through Noah, would the earth be more like G-d intended it to be?

The conclusion of this experiment was seen in the account of the tower of Babel in Genesis chapter 11. In this section, mankind desired to build a tower that would reach into the heavens with the objective of making a name for himself. It is also stated in this same section that mankind did not want to obey the L-rd's command to fill the earth. Hence, even when using the "best" man as the father of this new race of humans, the end result is the same—sinfulness. The reason for this failed experiment is obvious—Noah was also a descendant of Adam and therefore he, too, possessed a sinful nature. Immediately after the reader learns that man could not redeem himself, Abraham enters into the picture.

Theologians state that Abraham is synonymous with several religious concepts: promise, faith, and Israel. It is these three concepts that will provide the solution for man's sinful condition.

13

Promise

Now that it has been demonstrated in the Scripture that man is unable to provide redemption for himself, the gracious G-d performs two significant acts. The first of these is G-d's revelation of Himself to Abraham. The second is that He offered a conditional promise to Abraham. The condition of this promise was faith; that is, for the promise to be fulfilled, Abraham would have to respond to it by means of faith. If Abraham did so, then a new people would be established—the people of the Redeeming G-d, Israel.

Of what was this promise comprised? That G-d would make Abraham into a great nation, and through this people, all the families of the earth could be blessed (See Genesis 12:1-3). From this text the reader learns that G-d desires to bless mankind. Furthermore, the reader learns that G-d has a plan to carry out this desire and this plan centers on the people, i.e. the great nation, that would come from Abraham— Israel.

Perhaps here is a good time to be reminded that the L-rd is sovereign. He is free to determine the plan that He wants to use in order to offer redemption to mankind. Man is not in any position to either question this plan or believe that there should be any need for it to be changed. Before moving on, let us remember that the divine promise to bless man is inherently related to Israel, the people and the land ("*Go...to the land that I will show you*" Genesis 12:1).

Faith

The Bible reveals that G-d is gracious, in that He reveals Himself to man and His desire to bless man. Even though G-d is sovereign, man must respond to G-d by exercising faith. Faith is inherently related to Scripture; hence faith is when man responds to G-d in the manner which is revealed in the Word of G-d. Abraham believed G-d (Genesis 15:6) and the outcome was that G-d credited to him righteousness. This text teaches that because

Abraham responded to G-d in the way that the Word of G-d commanded, i.e. by means of faith, the outcome was that G-d considered Abraham to be righteous. Theologians state that by means of faith, G-d imputed righteousness upon Abraham.

It is most important to pay extra attention to a few of the words that the text uses in Genesis 15:6,

"And he (Abraham) *believed in the L-rd and He **calculated** it **for** him— righteousness."*

The Hebrew word which I translated *"calculated"* has an accounting quality to it. It should be understood as a transaction such as one depositing in the bank account of another a certain amount of money. Once the transaction is complete, the recipient is indeed the possessor of that which was credited to his account. Also note the word *"for"*. The intent of this word is to reveal to the reader that Abraham could not do this himself. In other words, Abraham could not ever become righteous had not G-d imputed it to him. Once again, that which was necessary for the transaction to be executed was faith. The Hebrew verb which appears in this text, which was translated *"believed"*, is derived from the same Hebrew root as the word *"faith"*. This verse also reveals that the outcome of G-d blessing man is a change in his spiritual status. Like Noah, and all descendants of Adam, man is sinful; but by means of the L-rd's promise to redeem man, he becomes righteous. Hence, the outcome of G-d blessing man is man who was lost and unable to redeem himself, becomes righteous—this is the blessing!

Israel

So far, in discussing the term "Israel", it was utilized as a people, the people of G-d who would descend from Abraham. However, in the Bible the term "Israel" can also be used in regard to land. Unfortunately many individuals, including a growing number of Christians, do not see the land of Israel as foundational in regard

15

to G-d's divine promise to bless man. Such a tendency ignores a great amount of Scripture and violates good hermeneutics.

All interpreters of the Bible see Genesis 15:6 as a highly significant verse, therefore it is necessary to also pay attention to what is revealed immediately after this statement. The next verse reads,

"And He said to him, I am the L-rd Who brought you from Ur Kasdim to give to you this land to inherit it." Genesis 15:7

Just as important in the Sovereign L-rd's plan of redeeming man and making him to be righteous, is G-d's gift of the land of Israel to the Jewish people. Ultimately the promises of G-d will not be realized until He establishes His Kingdom and one of the primary tenets of this book is that **the establishment of the Kingdom is dependent upon the Jewish people possessing the land that G-d gave to them.** Such a view is rare among the vast majority of individuals that call themselves Christian today. It virtually does not exist among the rest of the Gentiles and fewer and fewer of those of Jewish descent accept such a perspective. However truth is not dependent upon the majority, rather upon the Scripture alone.

Before entering into an overview of various Biblical texts that assert this tenet, first let's address to whom is the promise of the land given? Some mistakenly rush to answer this question by stating the sons of Abraham. Such an answer is not correct. If it were so, then Ishmael and his offspring would share equally in the promise. However, Scripture makes it clear that this is not the case.

"Drive out this female servant and her son, for the son of this female servant will not inherit with my son, with Isaac."
Genesis 21:10

Even though Sarah is the one who is speaking, G-d affirms these words in verse 12 of this passage. It is also significant that in the account of the offering of Isaac in Genesis 22, Isaac is called

Abraham's only son (See Genesis 22:2). Not only should one not include all of Abraham's sons as heirs to the promise of the land, one **cannot** include the sons of Isaac as well. If one includes Isaac's offspring, then Esau would have a right to the promise of the land of Israel, but his inheritance is the land of Edom (See Genesis 36:8). According to Scripture, it is not until one arrives at Jacob, that it is appropriate to attach the promise of the land to all his descendants.

Jacob, who is also called Israel, receives this promise along with his descendants in an interesting account from the Scripture. In Genesis chapter 28, Jacob is fleeing from his brother Esau, who intended to kill him (See Genesis 27:41) to the city of Haran. There his mother's family lived, and there he would marry and begat those who would become the tribes of Israel. It was during the initial days of his journey that Jacob had a dream. In this well known dream, a ladder appeared, reaching the heavens. This ladder is symbolically a type of "bridge" between the heavens and the earth. The text explicitly states that G-d spoke to Jacob and said,

"...I am the G-d of Abraham your father and the G-d of Isaac, the land which you are laying upon it, to you I will give it and to your descendants." Genesis 28:13

In this verse G-d identifies Himself in a unique way. He does so with a reference to Abraham and Isaac. Judaism teaches that when the Scripture references the Patriarchs, it is for the purpose of calling to the attention of the reader the covenantal promises which G-d first confirmed to Abraham and then to Isaac. Hence, in this section, G-d is extending the call which was upon Abraham and Isaac now to Jacob and his sons. Not only is the land mentioned in verse 13, but also in the following verse.

"And your offspring shall be as the dirt of the ground and you shall spread out to the west and to the east and to the north and to the south and shall be blessed in you all the families of the earth and in your offspring." Genesis 28:14

17

This verse makes it very clear that for the blessing G-d promises Abraham to become realized, the descendants of Jacob, the Jewish people, are integral. They must take possession of the land of Israel and dwell in it, in order for all the families of the earth to be blessed. In other words, the Kingdom which Messiah will establish will not come until Jewish individuals fulfill this commandment. This may be a new concept for many people and it may be difficult to hear such a bold statement and accept it from one verse. Therefore, this point will be developed in greater precision throughout this book. All I ask from the reader at this time is to be open and wait for greater support for it in the rest of Scripture.

In regard to the rest of this chapter, Jacob does a most unusual act. One must remember that this revelation came by means of a dream. In verse 11, Jacob selected from the stones of this place one on which he laid his head. Rabbinical scholars see the stone as related to the source of revelation which he received. Why is this? The answer is found in what Jacob does to the stone. Before answering this question, the reader must be reminded that Messiah is spoken about in the Scripture as a "rock" or "stone" (This point will be illustrated when Daniel chapter two is studied). After hearing the covenant promise being extended to him and its implications, Jacob anointed the stone with oil. The question that must be asked is why did Jacob do such a thing? As was previously pointed out by many of the Jewish commentators, the rock's connection to this revelation was now being acknowledged by Jacob in a special way. The fact that he anointed the rock with oil may in fact be a reference to Messiah, the L-rd's Anointed; however, the Hebrew word used in this verse in not the same word from which the term Messiah is derived. The point is that Jacob understood this promise as something which contained great significance and ultimately connected to the L-rd's plan of redemption. The New Testament also unites this passage with Yeshua's work of redemption. At the conclusion of John chapter 1 Jacob's ladder is referred to, but here instead of a ladder being mentioned, the ladder is replaced with the phrase, "*The Son of Man*", a clear reference to inform the reader that the true bridge between man and G-d is the Messiah (See John 1:43-51). The chapter concludes with this stone being promised to become the house of G-d, obviously a reference to worship. Before moving on to the next issue, allow me to state that the L-rd's plan of redemption, which is achieved by the work of Messiah, creates for man the ability to worship G-d as He desires.

Israel and the Jewish people are symbols the world is admonished to watch, in order to see the faithfulness of G-d. When Israel disobeyed G-d, He held her up before the world as a recipient of His divine judgment. However in the last days, Israel should be watched as a type of barometer for discerning the prophetic calendar. Matthew chapter 24 offers insight in regard to this assertion. When Yeshua spoke about the end times in this section He said,

"But from the fig tree learn the parable; whenever the branch becomes tender and the leaves are put forth, you know that near is the harvest. Thus also, you, whenever you should see all these things, know that it is near… at the door." Matthew 24:32-33

Since in the Bible Israel is likened to a fig tree, Messiah is instructing His followers to pay attention to what is going on in Israel. The word "parable" is used by Yeshua in order to instruct the reader that Israel must be observed with great attention. Parables were literary instruments that, when studied and if the proper hermeneutical rules are applied to them, they offer great insight. Hence, when one observes Israel in light of prophetic truth, a wealth of information is learned, leading to a better understanding of the last days.

The Apostle Paul spoke strongly about Israel and her relevance in the end times as well. It is clear that in Romans chapter 11 Paul anticipated that Israel, who for the most part had rejected the message of redemption through Yeshua, would in the last days come to faith. It is the outcome of this revival among Jewish individuals that Paul speaks of when he writes,

"But if their fall (be) the wealth of the world and their failure (be) wealth of the nations; how all the greater is their fullness." Romans 11:12

"For if their rejection (is) the reconciliation of the world, what (is) the receiving; except life from the dead." Romans 11:15

These two verses make it clear that because the vast majority of Jewish individuals have rejected the Gospel, numerous Gentiles have come to faith. As discussed earlier, the word which is translated *"nations"* in verse 12 actually has to do with ethnicities. This fact reveals that the Gospel is powerful to break through social barriers and touch the hearts of all individuals regardless race or any other social factor. Both of these verses teach that even though Israel's failure to respond properly to the Gospel had a positive effect in the world, their mass acceptance is going to have an even more dramatic outcome. What is this outcome? Paul states at the end of the 15th verse, *"life from the dead"*. This expression is a reference to the resurrection of the dead. Judaism, from the latter Second Temple period until today, sees an inherent relationship between the resurrection and the Kingdom. Hence, what Paul was teaching in this verse is that the Kingdom will not be established until there is a mass revival of Jewish individuals who turn to Yeshua as Savior.

Due to this fact, it should not be surprising that Satan would strongly oppose Israel and would want to hinder the Jewish people from embracing Yeshua. How will this opposition manifest itself? This is the subject of the next chapter.

Chapter 3

"Anti-Semitism: A Satanic Spirit"

Anti-Semitism is a controversial subject for some. Bring up the subject in a small group of people and immediately someone will point out that many other groups have suffered cruel atrocities as well. Sadly this is true, but the difference is that such atrocities are rooted in some type of historical dispute or conflict. Anti-Semitism is a feeling or action against a Jewish person or persons based only in the fact that one is Jewish. The root of Anti-Semitism is unexplainable from a rational standpoint, because it is spiritual in nature.

Throughout the Scripture, Anti-Semites have appeared and ultimately the one which Scripture calls the Anti-Christ, will rise to power for a period of time. He, according to Daniel, will bring about a second Holocaust more horrific than the first. There are certain names in the Bible which are synonymous with an Anti-Semitic spirit. One of the most infamous is Edom.

Edom

Edom has her origin in the book of Genesis. The Hebrew root from which the word "Edom" is derived means "red". The word is related to Jacob's brother Esau,

*"And the first one went out **reddish**, all of him, like a hairy garment, and they called his name Esau."* Genesis 25:25

The word which is translated "reddish" is the same word from which Edom originates. Later on in the same section of Genesis, Esau returns unsuccessfully from the field requesting from his brother, Jacob, a type of red stew. Once again, the word used twice here means "red" and is from the same Hebrew root. Due to this, Esau also became known as Edom (See Genesis 25:30).

21

Even though Esau is called Edom in this verse, throughout the Scripture Edom generally refers to the people who descended from Esau. An interesting characteristic concerning Edom is that Edom is a bloodthirsty people. Some scholars have asserted that this is why the color red is associated with her. Edom is mentioned many times throughout the Scripture and, apart from her love for war, she is usually seen opposing Israel and the will of G-d. Next a brief overview of Edom will be presented.

In considering first Esau, the reader learns that he is uninterested in the things of G-d. In spite of the fact that he is the firstborn of Isaac, the Scripture declares his hatred for this birthright, "...*and Esau despised the birthright.*" (See Genesis 25:34). The birthright was extremely significant, as it called the recipient to continue in the call that was upon Abraham and Isaac. Hence, Esau had the opportunity to walk in the heritage of the Patriarchs of Judaism and be used by G-d to bless others. The text reveals that such a call was not important to Esau, for he was willing to exchange participation in the L-rd's plan of redemption, a plan which at its very root was to bring blessing upon mankind, for one bowl of stew. Esau possessed a spirit that caused him to be used by Satan. When confronted with the call of the birthright he responded,

> "*And Esau said, 'behold I am going to die; and for what is this birthright to me.*" Genesis 25:32

Esau's statement shows that he was interested in only himself. It is this attitude that gives the enemy a foothold in one's life. What Esau was saying was that because he was going to die, the birthright was of no good to him. In other words, Esau had no belief in or concern for the future after his death. This means that Esau was not Kingdom-minded. Also notice how his response to G-d was so different from that of Abraham. When Abraham heard that G-d was offering him a leadership role in His plan of blessing others, Abraham departed to a land that he had never seen before. In other words, he exercised faith; whereas Esau, who saw no immediate benefit for himself, hated this call. The omniscient G-d, knowing Esau's character, prophesied to Rebecca, Esau's mother, that it would be the younger of the twins, Jacob, who would be the one who would carry on the Patriarchal call. Some see this interpretation as a violation of Romans 9:11. This verse points out G-d's selection of Jacob, rather than Esau, was not based upon works, for the call came upon Jacob before either were born. While this is true, the implications of Romans 9:11 do not mean that the Sovereign G-d is forbidden to use His omniscience and place a call based upon character and not works. The fact that G-d knew Jacob had a passion for the purposes of G-d, while Esau hated the things of G-d, could certainly figure into his call. One needs to remember the context for this section of Romans chapter 9 is not justification. As this section clearly states, it was not the works of Jacob that are being exalted here, but rather the perfect wisdom of the Omniscient G-d.

It is vital that the reader understand that the right of the firstborn contained a special blessing from the father. This blessing is critical for the one who possesses the birthright to carry out his commitment, and cannot be separated from the birthright. Careful study of Genesis chapter 27 reveals that although Esau had sold the birthright to Jacob, he still intended to be the recipient the blessing. This fact shows Esau's tendency to want to hinder Israel and the purposes of the living G-d. Such behavior characterizes Edom as well. In researching Edom further, one finds in his genealogy in Genesis 36, that Amalek was his descendant. This fact provides valuable information to the Bible student.

Amalek was also one who wanted to thwart G-d's purpose by hindering Israel. After Israel's great victory at the Red Sea, when the L-rd miraculously parted the sea for the Children of Israel to cross and then closed it upon the army of Pharaoh, Amalek appeared. The victory at the Red Sea made it clear that G-d's anointing was on Israel, but Amalek did not care. In fact, in speaking about the battle that took place one reads,

23

"Remember what Amalek did to you on the way when you departed from Egypt; when he happened to you on the way and attacked you at the rear (where) *all the weak ones after you* (were located) *you who were tired and weary and he did not fear G-d. And it shall come about when the L-rd your G-d gives to you rest from all your enemies around* (you) *in the land which the L-rd your G-d is giving to you to inherit it, you shall blot out the memory of Amalek from under the heavens—do not forget!"* Deuteronomy 25:17-19

Amalek knew that he could not defeat G-d's people, so he attacked at the rear of the camp where the weak, old, and weary would be located. In other words, he did not war against Israel to be triumphant, but simply to inflict suffering upon those who were least able to defend themselves. This is the Edomite spirit, a joy in seeing others suffer. It is for this reason that this passage commands the Children of Israel to utterly destroy Amalek. When will Israel fulfill this commandment? The answer is in the last days. There are two important clues which reveal to the reader that this battle will indeed occur just prior to the establishment of the Kingdom. The first is when the Scripture says *"And it shall come about when the L-rd your G-d gives to you rest from all your enemies...."* Since Israel was reestablished in 1948, this small country has been attacked several times. Currently Israel's neighbors are becoming more hostile in regard to her existence. Although there is much talk about a "peace plan" for bringing security to the Mideast, recent events seem to have only brought greater instability to this region and a greater likelihood for another war.

Therefore, the idea of Israel having rest from her enemies is something that will only take place during what the rabbis call, "Yamot HaMashiach", the days of Messiah. Hence Israel taking vengeance on Amalek will be an event that takes place immediately prior to Messiah beginning His thousand year reign from Jerusalem. The second clue that this is an end time's event is that no one knows who Amalek is today. Rabbinical scholars state that it will be Elijah the prophet who will return in the last days and make known to Israel the identity of Amalek.

In the same way that Amalek did not fear G-d, but moved to attack the weakest of the Children of Israel, so, too, did Edom. At the end of the First Temple period, Israel's behavior brought the judgment of G-d upon her. G-d raised up Nebuchadnezzar and the Babylonians. It was them who the L-rd called to place His judgment upon His people. However, Edom could not refrain from joining in and also exerting violence upon Israel. The prophet Obadiah says that G-d will severely chastise Edom for her actions (See Obadiah verses 10-18). In fact, this same prophet reveals that a war between Edom and Israel must occur prior to the Kingdom being established. We will look at this fact later in our study; now however, let us look at another incident concerning Amalek.

During the rule of King Saul, G-d commanded him to wage war upon Amalek and totally destroy not only all the people, but also all their possessions. Saul did not obey the L-rd's words, as he spared the best from Amalek's livestock and her king, Agag. Eventually Samuel the prophet carried out these instructions, but Saul's disobedience caused him to be rejected as king and during the delay in killing Agag, he fathered a child who carried on the people of Amalek so that eventually Agag's descendant, Haman, would rise to power and attempt to exterminate the Jewish people (See the book of Esther for the account of Haman's actions). The point which is clearly seen in Esau and the people that would come forth from him is that they would possess an irrational hatred for Israel and move over and over to attempt to thwart G-d's sovereign choice to use Israel to accomplish His plan to fulfill the Abrahamic Covenant. Although the Messiah is the ultimate fulfillment of how G-d used Israel in regard to the Abrahamic Covenant, prophecy demands that G-d will use Israel in other ways prior to the establishment of the Kingdom.

The Edomite spirit will grow in the last days and be a major reason for all the nations to attack Jerusalem (See Zechariah

14:2). Such animosity against Israel and the Jewish people is easily seen and growing in the world today.

Anti-Semitism and the World

After the world was forced to acknowledge the atrocities of the Holocaust, most reasonable people understood the need for a Jewish State. With England ending her colonization of what was called Palestine, a Jewish State was indeed established in her historical homeland. From the very beginning, the modern State of Israel was met with harsh opposition. Israel survived three major wars, Independence, Six Day, and Yom Kippur, in addition to other serious conflicts / wars and has achieved success that few other countries can match in a period of just over sixty years.

Although Israel has demonstrated a strong desire to be a friendly member of the international community, and has reached out frequently at times of need, far beyond that of her neighbors' participation in international relief efforts, the United Nations attempts to pass resolution after resolution against the tiny Jewish State. Had it not been for the general tendency of the United States to veto most of these resolutions, Israel would be in much more turmoil. Today the international community pressures Israel to make peace with those who have as their expressed goal her destruction. Due to such pressure, Israel pulled out of Southern Lebanon against her security needs and the terrorist organization Hezbollah stepped into the vacuum. A few short years later, after Hezbollah armed itself with rockets, war broke out. This war broke out after an Israeli patrol was ambushed by Hezbollah and several soldiers were killed.

A similar scenario happened a few years later after Israel had uprooted 8,000 citizens from the Gaza Strip in a good faith effort to make peace. Once again Israel's departure allowed other terrorist organizations, primarily Hamas, to arm themselves. Soon thereafter rockets smuggled in from Egypt began to be fired at Israeli citizens living in communities near Gaza. After absorbing nearly 8,000 rockets, and seeing the frequency rising to over 200 per week, Israel had no other option than to respond, after her warnings were ignored.

Once again the international community was quick to scold Israel and accuse her of gross human rights violations, which proved to be false. The question that needs to be asked is why was this same international community so silent during the unprovoked firing of rockets upon Israeli civilians? The world is silent concerning Israeli causalities, but when Israel responds in defense of her citizens, the world rushes to urge Israel to show restraint. Where were the resolutions at the UN against Hezbollah, Hamas, and other terrorist organizations who claimed responsibility? Any objective individual who examines the international community's behavior in regard to Israel has to acknowledge a double standard against the Jewish State. What is the basis for such a double standard? The answer is the Edomite spirit.

The Edomite Spirit

Psalm 137 is a special psalm in Judaism. On normal days after one eats a meal, the prayer which is said in order to thank the L-rd for His provision begins with this psalm. In verse seven one reads,

"*Remember O L-rd the sons of Edom, on the day of Jerusalem, the ones who said, 'destroy destroy unto its foundation.*'"

It is significant in this psalm that not only does Edom hate Israel, but also she places herself against the G-d of Israel. From where in this verse is such an assertion derived? The Scripture states that Jerusalem is the place where G-d caused His name to dwell (Deuteronomy 16:2, 6). Therefore, wanting to see and taking part in the destruction of Jerusalem and the Temple, is tantamount to setting oneself against the L-rd. Notice that this seventh verse is in stark contrast to the psalmist's great love for the Holy City.

The Edomite spirit will cause one to oppose the Messiah as well. In the Book of Lamentations, which also laments the destruction the Temple, one encounters a very important verse concerning Messiah.

"The spirit of our nostrils is the L-rd's Messiah. He was caught in their pits; (about) *Whom we said, 'in His shadow we will live among the nations."* Lamentations 4:20

In order to understand the intent of Jeremiah (the traditional author of Lamentations), one must pay close attention to the phrase, *"the spirit of our nostrils"*. This is a reference to the creation of man, for in the Book of Genesis one learns that what caused the dirt which G-d had fashioned to become a living soul is when He breathed into Adam's nostrils (See Genesis 2:7). What is the relationship between this reference and the Messiah? Jeremiah is communicating to the reader that one should view the Messiah as the Giver of life. In the next part of the verse, one reads that Messiah has died. The phrase, *"He was caught in their pits"* refers to death, as the word translated "pits" is frequently used in a parallel manner to the grave (See Psalm 16:10). Hence Jeremiah is likening the destruction of Jerusalem to that of the crucifixion of Yeshua. It was the Messiah Whom the people thought would grant them security to live among the nations, but now with His death, the hope that Israel had was being challenged.

As believers, we know Messiah's horrific death, which Satan rejoiced over, actually became the means of victory. In a similar manner, those in the last days who go up to Jerusalem to destroy the Holy City, will actually be fulfilling what the L-rd says has to happen for the Kingdom to come. However, those who do so will not be rewarded for moving the events of the prophetic timeline forward, for their actions were not motivated in obedience; but rather by hatred for Israel and the things of G-d. The same thing could be said about Nebuchadnezzar and the Babylonians who waged war against Israel, not due to any righteous reason, but due to their own greed, selfishness, and barbaric nature.

It is of course not a coincidence that in the next verse Edom is mentioned,

"*Rejoice and be glad O daughter of Edom, who dwells in Utz; unto you the cup will pass, you will become drunk and will be destroyed.*" Lamentations 4:21

Whereas Israel is saddened over Messiah's death, Edom rejoices. Once again this verse shows how over and over Edom stands in opposition to the things of G-d. The land of Utz is a region in Southeast Jordan. The second half of the verse makes it clear that Edom will be punished. The same word which is used to depict her final condition, "*destroyed*", is the same word used in Psalm 137 when Edom wanted the foundation of Jerusalem to be laid to waste, "*destroy destroy unto its foundation*". The same word can be translated with the idea "*making one naked*". Therefore it is not simply a matter of destruction, as I have translated, but there is also a nuance of shame involved. The same word is used in both texts to show that what Edom wanted to happen to Jerusalem and to the purposes of G-d, will in fact actually be visited upon Edom.

Anti-Semitism and the Church

The purpose of this section is not to provide the reader with an historical overview of the numerous acts of persecution that the Church has inflicted upon the Jewish people. Hence the Crusades, the Inquisition, and the overwhelming silence and even participation of "Christianity" during the Holocaust will not be discussed. Rather, in this section a brief look at a growing trend in theology will be addressed. This theology empties the Bible of most of its promises to Israel and ignores numerous prophecies concerning the role Israel will play in the last days. A popular Christian pastor who expounds this view is John Piper of Bethlehem Baptist church in Minneapolis, Minnesota. Before discussing this theology in particular, let us see how such a theology shapes one's view concerning the modern State of Israel.

Rev. Piper, in his article "*Israel, Palestine and the Middle East*" (this article is available on DesiringGod.org) writes,

"*The existence of Israel in the Middle East and the extent of her borders and her sovereignty are perhaps the most explosive factors in world terrorism and the most volatile factors in Arab-West relations.*"

Why would Rev. Piper say that Israel's existence is the most explosive factor in world terrorism? Obviously what takes place in Israel at the hands of Palestinian terrorists is of course related to Israel. However, the numerous other acts of terrorism that unfortunately occur throughout the world are not at all related to Israel's existence. When a person asserts such a claim, he is simply repeating the rhetoric of those who want to delegitimize Israel's existence. In other words, Rev. Piper has accepted the propaganda of Palestinian media outlets that want to blame Israel for most of the world's problems as a means of fulfilling their desire to undermine Israel's right to exist. A similar strategy was utilized by Hitler when he blamed the Jewish people for most of the problems confronting Germany.

As in Rev. Piper's article, this view that Israel's existence is a destabilizing factor in the world and causes the United States of America to have poor relations with the Arab world, must be examined. It is the assertion of this writer that the growth of Islam and the fact that more and more countries in the Middle East are either now ruled by a Muslim government or being greatly influenced by Islam is the real reason why there is instability in the Middle East and growing tensions between the West and the Arab world. In the next chapter the problem with Islam will be addressed. However now, it must be stated that poor theology has caused a growing number of Christian leaders to embrace views hostile to Israel and the Jewish people.

At the heart of this theology are two major tenets. **The first is because the overwhelming majority of Jewish individuals have rejected Yeshua as the Messiah, Israel has lost her right to the land and the second is that the Church replaces Israel as the people of G-d.** This is known as replacement theology.

In regard to the first assumption, there is no Scriptural foundation for such a theological perspective at all. There is no place in the Word of G-d where the right to the land of Israel is dependent upon faith in Yeshua. Of course disobedience to His commandments is clearly a basis for Israel being sent into exile. Therefore could not one rightly conclude that rejecting Yeshua is disobedience and as an outcome of this disobedience Israel was sent into exile? Yes one could and he would be correct. However this is not what is being asserted by Rev. Piper and others. There is a very significant difference; Israel going into exile is not the same thing as losing the right to the land permanently, thereby making it available to others.

Here is a silly example to help illustrate the difference. When I was a child I received a very nice bicycle from my parents. I loved riding the bicycle and took great delight in knowing it was mine. One day I disobeyed my father and I lost my right to ride the bicycle for a period of time. Eventually the punishment came to an end and I once again was riding my bicycle. It would be quite a different thing for my father, instead of setting my bicycle aside for a week, to give it to another child. Yes, Israel has acted in disobedience by not applying prophetic truth to Yeshua and reaching the conclusion that He is indeed the Messiah. Yes, Israel went into exile for a very long period of time. However there is no Scriptural foundation for believing that the covenantal promise of the Land of Israel, which G-d has given to the Jewish people, has been lost. In fact, Paul writes in regard to Israel,

"For the gifts and the calling of G-d are unchangeable."
Romans 11:29

One should pay close attention to the word translated as "unchangeable". The first letter of this Greek word is actually a prefix which changes the meaning of the word from that which was possible to now something which is impossible. According to the Harold K. Moulton's Greek lexicon the word means, "To change one's judgments on past points of conduct; to change one's mind and purpose". Hence, because of the prefix attached to the word, it now strongly asserts that G-d has not changed His plan, purpose or calling in regard to Israel or the Jewish people. How sure can one be of this? The writer of Hebrews uses the same word in regard to the oath that G-d has made to Yeshua that He is a Priest forever of the order of Malchizedek (See Hebrews 7:21). Therefore, if the promise G-d made to the Jewish people can be rendered void, then believers would have no assurance that Yeshua might not one day be replaced with another "Messiah".

The fact of the matter is that there are numerous prophecies which affirm that in the end times Jewish people will be reestablished in the land and possess it as a non-negotiable prerequisite for the Kingdom to come. Furthermore, there are two wonderful outcomes to the Jewish people returning to their land. The first is, whereas in times past the vast majority of Jewish people have rejected Yeshua, back in their land in the last days, the vast majority of Jewish individuals will accept Him as Messiah. The second outcome is that when the Gentiles see the faithfulness of G-d as has been expressed to the Jews, there will also be a great number of them as well who will accept Yeshua. The final chapter of this book is dedicated to such prophecies.

In addressing whether the Jewish people are still the people of G-d or not, some foundational theological truths must be set forth first. The most important of these is that salvation, i.e. redemption, is only by means of Yeshua. That is, only His death on the cross, and the shedding of His blood, provide the necessary payment for sin. Without an acceptance of Him, based on faith, one is lost. No group of people receives a pass from the absolute necessity of receiving Yeshua as one's personal Savior, not the Jews, not anyone.

When a Gentile places his faith in Yeshua, he too shares in the promises of the Kingdom just like any Jew who receives Him. G-d is not a respecter of persons. However, the call of the Church and the call of Israel have some different aspects to them. The Church, for example, has a clear calling to provoke Israel to jealousy (Romans 11:11). This means that believers have had a calling placed upon them to live in such a way, by means of their salvation experience, that Jewish individuals would want that same experience. I fully accept that Christians are the people of G-d. This fact is simply the realization of what G-d said to Abraham,

> *"I, behold My covenant is with you; and you shall become a father to many nations."* Genesis 17:4

Again, regardless of ethnicity or nationality, all who believe in Yeshua become part of the family of G-d. Yet, there remains a distinct identity for the physical descendants of Jacob as the "people of G-d". Failure to understand this point has brought theological error into the Church and was the basis for some of the most shameful chapters of Christian history.

Two favorite passages that replacement theologians like to use, in an attempt to justify their position, are Matthew 21 and John 8.

Matthew 21:33-46

In this section Yeshua tells a parable. This parable is of a man who planted a vineyard and prepared it so that a business could be managed from it. This man leased it out to another. At the time when the vineyard produced its fruit, this man sent his servants to collect his portion of the harvest. Instead of responding according to the agreement, the man that was in charge of the vineyard beat or even killed the ones the owner would send in order to collect his portion. Finally the owner sent his son, thinking that he would be respected and the terms of the agreement would be fulfilled. Because the son was the natural heir to the vineyard, the man who was tending the vineyard believed that killing him would gain for him the vineyard.

In this parable, the owner of the vineyard represents G-d and the one who was placed in charge of the vineyard represents some of the chief priests and Pharisees. The servants who were either beaten or killed represent the prophets and the son of the vineyard owner represents Yeshua. **The error that many make in interpreting this parable is to liken the man who tended the vineyard and killed the servants and owner's son to the Jewish people in general or to the nation of Israel.** Such a conclusion is absolutely incorrect. The text itself affirms that the parable was addressed only to the chief priests and Pharisees who were there.

"And hearing, the chief priest and the Pharisees His parable; they knew that concerning them He speaks." See Matthew 21:45.

Also in this parable Yeshua states to those leaders,

"On account of this I say to you that will be lifted from you the Kingdom of G-d and it will be given a nation bearing its fruits." Matthew 21:43

Is it correct to interpret this verse in regard to the land of Israel? The answer is **no**, because the subject of the verse is the Kingdom and not the land. Nor is it proper to apply this parable to the Jewish people's status as the people of G-d, because the Jewish people in general are not ever mentioned in this parable. The correct interpretation is that the preaching of the means by which one enters into the Kingdom of G-d, i.e. the Gospel of the Messiah, would not be done by Israel's leaders, but a different nation (literally ethnic group) would be given this responsibility. Has this not come about as now it is primarily Gentiles who have been the preachers of the Gospel and not Judaism or its leaders for nearly the last 2,000 years?

Rev. Piper, like many other Replacement theologians, uses this text (See the aforementioned article or his 2004 message with the same title) as a basis for saying,

"Israel has broken covenant with G-d...therefore, the secular state of Israel today may not claim a present divine right to the land."

Such a conclusion goes well beyond the scope of this passage and cannot be supported in the Scripture.

John Chapter 8

In this chapter, Yeshua enters into a dialogue with some of the Pharisees and, once again, not the Jewish people in general. Therefore, it is hermeneutically incorrect to apply the statements that Yeshua made in this chapter to anyone other than to this particular group of Pharisees. Rev. Piper is not alone in his rush to label all Jews with the words that Yeshua spoke to a few. In the same article / sermon he states in his discussion of John chapter 8,

"But Israel does not love Jesus as God's son and her Messiah. So they are, for now, 'enemies of God.'"

Why do those who embrace Replacement theology fail to include in their discussion of this chapter that many Jews, upon hearing Yeshua's teaching believed on Him,

"As He spoke these things many believed in Him. Therefore Yeshua spoke to the Jews who believed in Him..."
                                                        John 8:30-31a

Perhaps there were more Jewish individuals who believed in Yeshua that day than Pharisees who rejected Him. How does Rev. Piper arrive at the conclusion that Israel (his intent is Jews in general) is the enemy of G-d and loses claim on to land of Israel. Sadly, most people will reject the Gospel, for Yeshua taught that the way into the Kingdom is narrow and few find it (Matthew

7:14). So, because a majority of mankind will reject the Gospel, those who do believe lose their right to enter into the Kingdom? Obviously not; so, because a majority of Jews reject Yeshua, the Jewish people in totality forfeit their claim to the land of Israel? The fact of the matter is there is not any Scripture that links the rejection of Yeshua to the Jewish people's loss of the land. On the contrary, as will be demonstrated later on in this book, G-d will keep His covenant with the Jewish people concerning the land, and as a result of this, He will move to complete His program of redemption.

It is most disturbing that more and more Christians are advocating a two state solution which would create an Islamic state in the very place that was the Biblical heartland of Israel. What are the implications of this from both a secular and a Scriptural point of view? This is in what the following chapter shall engage.

Chapter 4

"The Growth of Islam…should one be concerned?"

Which religion is the largest? If one includes Catholicism with Christianity, then Islam is the second largest religion in the world. When trying to discern which religion is the fastest growing, it can be somewhat more difficult to determine. However, if one simply looks at the number of adherents, Islam is growing faster than any other religion. Those who argue that Islam is not the fastest growing religion point out that this is because Islam is the prevalent religion in some of the fastest growing countries in the world. Also, Muslim families have a very high birth rate that skews the numbers. However, when looking at new converts, that is, people who profess no religion or a different one and then converts to either Islam or Christianity, Christianity is growing faster than Islam. But, if one simply asks the question how many adherents there are to a particular religion in the world on January 1, and then compare that number to December 31, the greatest increase will be in Islam. Another significant characteristic of these two major religions is that Muslims are growing more committed to their religion, while Christians are becoming more nominal in their observance. It is this latter tendency of Islam that will be the primary focus of this chapter.

Islam and its followers

Islam is changing in regard to its demands upon its followers. The level of commitment that is being required today is much greater than historically was demanded. Muslims have become much more visible in society as the basic rules of dress for women have drastically been altered. Men, too, are displaying in a variety of different ways, a greater level of observance. Islamic law (Sharia), which was often ignored by a majority of Muslims, is now being taught and embraced by an ever-increasing percentage of

Muslims. The requirements of Sharia law are what define a Muslim community today. What do these changes mean for those who are not Muslims?

At first, Islam teaches that as a minority within a community, they must not make demands upon those who are not part of their religion and they keep their religious practices quietly and non-obtrusively. However, when their community grows in number and becomes a significant percentage (although still a minority), more and more demands and expectations are required by Muslims from those who are not adherents to Islam. At first such demands are often agreed to as an effort by non-Muslims in order to be sensitive and considerate to their Muslim neighbors. However, as Islamic influence grows in a community, so, too, does the extent and tone of their demands. As their expectations become more infringing upon non-Muslims, there reaches a point when non-Muslims will refuse to comply with such demands. This refusal is usually met by Muslims with protests which often times become violent and destructive to property.

This response reveals Islam's willingness to embrace violence and intimidation to bring about its objectives. Such behavior is not only condoned, but taught as legitimate expressions of service to the Muslim god, Allah. When one examines terrorism throughout the world, he will discover that a very high percentage is committed by Muslims. It is not only for compliance with Sharia law that violence is carried out, but also to suppress the expression of other religions. In Muslim countries it is increasingly common for terrorism to be committed against Christians and for churches to be destroyed. In fact, in places where Sharia law is the law of the country, individuals that embrace a religion other than Islam are arrested and executed. Such facts are not new information for most individuals. So why discuss them here? It is important because of the distortion by Western media.

When terrorism takes place, the Western media cannot state fast enough that such acts of violence should not be linked to Islam, but rather to a few Muslim extremists that do not represent Islam in general. This simply is false! The facts reveal a much different picture of Islam. For example, on December 21, 1988, Pan Am flight 103 was brought down by a bomb planted in a suitcase. Abdelbaset Al-Megrahi was convicted of the crime. Although he was given a life sentence for his crime, he was released on August 20, 2009, on so-called humanitarian grounds. When arriving in Libya as a free man, he received a hero's welcome and Muslim clerics were present in large numbers, kissing him and speaking at his reception and praising his action. Where was the condemnation for this man from the Muslim community? It simply did not exist. When terrorism happens, Muslims across the world rejoice as was seen on September 11, 2001. Media outlets briefly broadcasted Palestinian Muslims dancing and cheering in the streets in celebration of nearly the 4,000 innocent individuals who lost their lives, until then-Prime Minister Yasser Arafat closed down such broadcasts. It is important to note that such celebrations took place throughout the Muslim world. Once again, where were the condemnations by the leading Muslim clerics of these heinous crimes? They did not exist.

Although Muslim religious leaders will publically praise acts of terrorism, often Muslim political leaders will issue statements of condemnation in English; however, in Arabic they issue praise for them. This is the standard behavior of Palestinian politicians when a terrorist act is carried out against Israeli civilians. Those who killed by means of strapping a bomb to their bodies and blowing themselves up, killing numerous innocent civilians, are called martyrs and hailed as heroes. Their pictures are hung in public places as an encouragement to others, usually the youth, in order to influence them to do the same. The point that must be acknowledged is that this is not the attitude of a few misguided individuals who are attempting to hijack one of the great world religions, but rather the teaching of true Islam.

When looking at the origin of Islam, one finds that Muhammad used violence to secure Islam as the dominant religion of the Arab Peninsula. His followers would raid villages, inflicting death and violence upon individuals and gain wealth and power. It was based upon the physical struggle that early Islam used to gain power that the concept of Jihad entered into Islam. This concept legitimizes the use of force in order to secure the objectives of Islam. Today, many argue about the true meaning and proper application of the term Jihad. Some have argued that it should not be applied to a physical conflict, but rather refers to a personal inner struggle of an individual. In other words, some have likened Jihad to one's personal struggle with temptation and strongly disagree with those who use it to justify terrorism or any other physical act of violence. So who is right concerning this issue?

Perhaps an example from the Jewish world might assist one in understanding the essence of the issue. In speaking about Judaism, one may be referring to historical Judaism, i.e. Orthodox Judaism, or a newer expression called Reform Judaism. The differences between these two shed light on Islam. Orthodox Judaism applies sacred religious texts, such as the Talmud and the Hebrew Bible, upon its followers as binding. Whereas in Reform Judaism, there are no binding texts placed upon its followers. In other words, Reform Judaism is more of a cultural expression that celebrates a heritage, than a truly religious expression. Primary acts of observance such as the Sabbath, Kashrut (dietary laws), and family purity are rejected by Reform Judaism, leaving the individual free to decide how his "religion" impacts his life. Reform rabbis tend not to bring to their parishioners sermons rooted in religious texts, but sermons based in social concerns where human reason forms the basis for the rabbis' views and not any authoritative texts.

So, too, in the minds of some Muslims, is the Koran. These individuals may call themselves Muslim, but are hardly followers of Islam; no more than a Reform Jew practices a Torah-based Judaism. It is this type of "Muslim" who identifies himself or herself as a Muslim only for cultural reasons, rather than any commitment to the teachings of the Koran. When confronted with passages from the Koran which condone violence, this person is forced to allegorize them, rather than understand them in the manner in which they are presented. In short, when one evaluates Islam, based upon the teachings of the Koran and other authoritative texts, one must conclude that Islam is a violent religion which must be seen as a great threat to the freedom of others. It is therefore most unusual that few individuals in leadership positions in Western society will admit the threat of Islam or take the necessary precautions and actions to properly deal with it. Why is this?

Islamic Distortions

Islam has utilized media in a very beneficial manner in order to move forward in obtaining its goals. Recruitment of new converts is a primary objective of Islam. In the West, where Judeo-Christian beliefs are prevalent, Islam takes great pride in promoting itself as a monotheistic religion. Although this is true, one should not be confused into believing that the Muslim god Allah is the same G-d revealed in the Old and New Testaments. Islam would never assert that Allah is the G-d of Israel. It cannot because the characteristics, attributes, and teachings of the Judeo-Christian G-d are vastly different from that of Allah. Muslims among themselves readily acknowledge this, yet because the Koran includes some of the same people as in the Judeo-Christian Bible, Moses and Yeshua for example, many in the West assert that Muslims worship the same G-d.

Yeshua of Nazareth is distorted in the Koran to be far less than that of what the New Testament reveals. This is true for all the common material between that of the Koran and the Judeo-Christian Scriptures. For example, it is not Isaac that Abraham is called to sacrifice, but Ishmael. Careful study of the Koran reveals that material from the Bible was included in the Koran as a cognitive attempt to ease the transition for those that came from other religions. Today this is being utilized with great success, as Islamic outreach in the African-American community, which has traditionally been Christian, is becoming more and more Islamic. Church buildings in major urban areas are becoming mosques because a majority of those who attend have accepted Islam as their new religion.

Within Christianity itself, many have embraced the identity of Yeshua, that He is the Son of Allah, justifying such blasphemy by stating that Allah simply is the generic name of G-d in Arabic. Whereas in Semitic languages the root for G-d is related to the Arabic word Allah, it is a distortion of the Scriptural witness to use the phrase "Yeshua, the Son of Allah", because in Islamic culture, Allah only refers to the Muslim deity to which Muhammad is his prophet. Because the Muslim deity is vastly different from the true G-d of the Judeo-Christian Scriptures, it is linguistically incorrect to use such an expression because it misleads those who are hearing it into believing something that is Biblically false.

Islam reaches out to make converts for several reasons; the primary one is to gain control of a region. One must not lose sight that when peaceful methods do not accomplish this objective, violence will be utilized. A cursory look at much of the Middle East supports this view. Islamic movements are gaining power in many countries and more and more representation in Middle East and Asia governments is Islamic. Many countries have been spared of violence, simply because the governments do not move against their endeavors. Islam has used freedoms and governmental procedures to their advantage, only to remove such freedom after gaining power. Afghanistan, under the Taliban, is an excellent example of this. When Islamic rule has the support of the government, terrorist organizations surface and recruitment ceases to be based in an ideological agreement, but is coerced by force.

The Middle East in transition

The spring of 2011 has seen much turmoil in many countries in the Middle East. Protests and uprisings calling for political change and human rights have surfaced, many successfully bringing about change in political leadership. Many in the West support these efforts and liken them to America's own struggle for independence. Such views are incorrect and demonstrate a naivety for what is occurring in the region. Iran's supreme leader was quoted in late February of 2011, during a speech given to clerics at an international Islamic conference held in Tehran, as saying, "The uprisings in the Arab world are Islamic,... the enemies are trying to portray the popular movement in the Muslim world as non-Islamic, when it is clear that it is completely Islamic and must be supported."

This comment was made prior to strong opposition and demonstrations in Syria against her leader Bashar Al-Assad, who is a close ally of Iran. Because of this relationship, the support for the protest and uprising being voiced in Iran has been tempered. The situation in Syria is somewhat of an abnormality. Although many of the ones who have taken to the streets in the Middle East during the Spring of 2011 were truly seeking freedom and human rights, Muslim organizations were quick to join in and, due to their resources and the fact that they were well organized, they were able to exploit and utilize these protests and the changes which they brought about for their own political gains. Although much is still in transition at the time of this writing, already in Egypt the new government is rethinking its peace agreement with Israel and making changes at the border between Egypt and Gaza. These changes at the border compromise Israeli security, as many of the weapons that the terrorist organization Hamas acquires are brought through this border crossing.

The Al-Assad rule in Syria, father and now son, was not so much rooted in Islamic ideology, but their administration needed the backing of Islamic leaders to maintain its rule. Naturally, the military plays a major role in continuing this oppressive government. The Al-Assad rule was forced to tolerate numerous terrorist organizations based in Syria in order to survive. Iran utilizes Syria as a pawn, but one should not be mistaken; when Bashar Al-Assad falls, Iran will see to it that a truly Islamic ruler takes control of the new Syrian government. Whether relatively peacefully as in Turkey, or by means of intimidation as Hezbollah has done to increase her influence in Lebanon, Islamic regimes are an ever-increasing reality in the Middle East and Asia. Some in Europe have a growing concern, but there is still a great hesitancy among its leaders to call Islam what it is—a violent movement rooted more in political power than anything related to a true religious expression. So why is Islam growing so rapidly in the world?

Islam has a history of thriving when there is poverty and the lack of educational opportunities. The language of the Koran is a much higher form of the various Arabic dialects spoken throughout the Arab world. The vast majority of Arabs is unable to read the Koran and must rely upon the teaching of their clerics in order to understand the message of Islam. Most in the West do not realize that Islam is an evolving religion and new decrees of certain clerics become just as binding as the Koran itself. The East is going through a major transformation that is spreading its influence and presence into the West. The handwriting is on the wall for those who are willing to read it—a major war is on the horizon. Such previous conflicts as in Iraq, Afghanistan, Libya etc., have only one purpose in the Islamic mind: a new strategy for war.

Islam's War Plan

Although the Arab world is not the best educated, the lack of formal education should not lead one to conclude that Arabs are not intelligent. Nothing could be further from the truth. Moreover, one of the most positive traits that the Muslim world has is patience. Muslims know that fighting the West, namely the United States of America, in a traditional military conflict will not lead to a successful conclusion. America's military strength simply cannot be matched by even an Islamic confederation of armies. Muslim leaders are certainly aware of this and their war on the West has taken this into consideration. America is such a super power because of her wealth. Hence, Islam is attacking America at her source of power, her financial wellbeing.

Since the late 1980's, America has spent an ever-increasing amount of money each year on her security needs. Today armed conflicts, such as the wars in Iraq and Afghanistan, are tremendous financial drains on the U.S. economy. These conflicts are not examples of traditional wars, as the constant occurrence of Muslim-based terrorist acts have proven to be highly successful in causing America to continue her costly operations for extended periods of time. In spite of her military superiority, and the numerous victories on the ground, the threat level that originates from these countries has not been noticeably impacted. It is precisely because of this that American foreign policy has been altered to where it is not only about destroying the enemy—who is often times very difficult to identify as we are not fighting a traditional army—but to establish democratic regimes in these countries that will move against the terroristic threats. These nation-building efforts, unfortunately, will probably turn out with the same degree of success as when the Taliban gained control in Afghanistan; having been backed, at least indirectly, by the U.S. "Ahmed Rashid, a leading author and expert on Afghan affairs, said it was "clear" that Washington, which armed and trained the Afghan mujahedin during their battle against Soviet invaders in the 1980s, indirectly supported the Taliban. 'The United States encouraged Saudi Arabia and Pakistan to support the Taliban, certainly right up to their advance on Kabul' on September 26, 1996, ... 'That seems very ironic now.'" (From an article by Phillip Knightley in the Guardian, October 8, 2001).

Islam's continued growth and influence in the world will not lessen any time soon. In fact, I would not be the first to assert that Islam will play a major role in the last days.

Chapter 5

"The Beast in the Last Days"

Daniel was a great man of G-d who received visions and the ability to interpret dreams. In the book that bears his name, the king of Babylon, Nebuchadnezzar, dreamed a dream which has great significance for the end times. This dream consisted of an image, a huge statue of sort, whose head was gold, chest and arms were silver, midsection and thighs were bronze, legs were iron and feet were a mixture of iron and clay. Daniel makes it clear that each section represents a different empire. The first empire, or kingdom, is that over which Nebuchadnezzar himself ruled, i.e. Babylon. The next is the empire of the Medes and Persians. The third is that of Greece while the fourth is Rome. It is the fifth kingdom, consisting of iron and clay, which will prove to be unique from all others. It is most significant that these kingdoms are revealed in one image. This is because each of these empires shared a common characteristic; they were opposed to the purposes of G-d. This fact is established when Daniel interprets the portion of Nebuchadnezzar's dream which spoke of a stone.

> "And you saw until a stone was cut without human hands, it struck the image at its feet of iron and clay and broke them to bits. They were broken together; the iron, the clay, the bronze, the silver and the gold. And they became like chaff from a summer threshing floor and the wind lifted them up and there did not remain any trace of them. And the stone that struck the image became a great mountain and filled all the earth." Daniel 2:34-35

There are many vital pieces of information contained in this short passage. The first is that most Biblical scholars understand the "stone" mentioned here as a reference to the Messiah. This means that, although Messiah will strike at the feet of the image, i.e. the foundation, the entire image will be destroyed. Next, due to the fact that Messiah will strike the fifth empire, one can conclude that this kingdom, which is represented by the legs and the feet, will not arise until the end times. Finally, it is Messiah Who will become a great kingdom and rule over the entire earth. This is because the term "mountain" in the Scriptures, when used symbolically, refers to a seat of government. This point is also supported later on in Daniel's interpretation of the dream when he states,

"And in the days of these kingdoms, the G-d of heavens will establish a kingdom that will never be destroyed, this kingdom will not pass to another people, it will break into pieces all these kingdoms and place upon them their end and will be established forever." Daniel 2:44

These empires are a subject that Daniel deals with in several different places in his prophecy. Daniel chapter seven is another such place. In this section a new king, Belshazzar, is ruling over Babylon. It was during his administration that Daniel himself had a dream. The dream begins with a vision of the four winds of heaven blowing upon the Great Sea—the Mediterranean Sea. The number four in Hebrew numerology has a global aspect to it; therefore, this dream pertains to something that will impact the entire world. The term "wind" often times speaks of a change or transition; hence this dream is about something which will bring about change and a transition in the world. When a sea is referenced in apocalyptic literature, it is a way of depicting instability, as the sea is constantly moving. Therefore, Daniel's dream speaks to a change that will affect the entire world; it will bring about a transition that will be caused by an initial period of global instability.

Next, there are four beasts mentioned in this passage. These beasts represent empires or kingdoms. There is a relationship between Nebuchadnezzar's dream in chapter two and that of Daniel's in chapter seven. The first beast is described to be like a lion. Most scholars associate this beast with Babylon. The second beast is likened to a bear. The consensus concerning this beast is that it represents the Persian Empire. The third beast is said to be like a leopard. It is the Greek Empire which this animal portrays. The final beast is different from those that came before it. No specific animal is named; however, three important adjectives are used to describe this beast. The reader is told that it is exceedingly horrific, terrible and strong. This beast also had large teeth of iron by which it was able to bring about great destruction. It also used its feet to trample that which was not destroyed with its teeth. The reader is also informed that this beast had ten horns. This fourth beast is said to represent the Roman Empire.

It has already been stated that there exists a relationship between the dreams of Nebuchadnezzar and Daniel. This being the case, one must ask the question why Nebuchadnezzar's dream consisted of five kingdoms while Daniel's had only four. This is most problematic when, later on in chapter seven, it would seem that after the defeat of Daniel's fourth beast the Messianic Kingdom is established. In other words, Nebuchadnezzar's dream has five empires ruling prior to Messiah's coming, while Daniel's dream only has four. The solution is that the Roman Empire will appear twice. This fact is hinted to in Nebuchadnezzar's dream by the revelation that his fourth kingdom consists of iron, while the fifth is a mixture of iron and clay. Hence, iron is mentioned in both empires in order to show a relationship between them.

Concerning this beast which represents Rome, special attention is given to its ten horns. It was precisely because of these horns, and an additional horn which would surface later, that Daniel is highly intrigued. This additional horn, which is said to be smaller than the others, uproots three of the ten horns when he arises. One learns later on in this same chapter (See verse 24) that each horn represents a king or kingdom. That is, that a future empire related to that of the ancient Roman Empire will arise in the last days and this empire will consist of ten nations or kingdoms. During this empire's rule, an additional king will arise and this one will be different from each of the previous ten. He will subdue three of the ten kings and take leadership of this empire (See verses 23-24). This king will speak blasphemous words against G-d and wage war against the followers of G-d. His rule will be for a time and times and a half time, or three and a half years (See verse 25). It is said of this one that he will want to alter the calendar and laws (also in verse 25). This chapter ends with a promise from G-d that this one will be destroyed and the eternal Kingdom of the Living G-d will be established.

The book of Revelation also speaks of this vision, adding some clarifying information. In chapter 17 of this book, a harlot is seen sitting on many waters. The expression "*many waters*" in the book of Revelation refers to a great amount of people (See Revelation 17:15 and 19:6). Therefore this harlot rules over most of the world. Throughout the Hebrew Scriptures, harlotry is usually a reference to idolatry or improper worship. What the text is therefore saying is that in the end times the vast majority of people will not be worshipping the G-d of Israel, but will be engaged in idolatrous worship. It is very significant that the reader is told that this harlot sits upon a beast (See verse 3). In other words, since a beast represents a world empire, idolatrous worship will characterize the final empire that will arise in the world prior to the establishment of the Kingdom of G-d. In this same verse, the beast is said to be scarlet, a color that represents sin (See Isaiah 1:18). This beast is full of names of blasphemy which is similar to Daniel 7:25 in that it has seven heads and ten horns. Later on in this chapter, the reader receives an interesting explanation concerning the beast.

"*...The seven heads are seven mountains which the woman sits upon and they are seven kings; five have fallen, one is and the other has not yet come and whenever he shall come, a little while it is necessary for him to remain.*"

Revelation 17:9-10

In this passage one learns that the seven heads are mountains. It has already been stated that in eschatological literature a mountain is related to a government or rule. Hence, this beast represents seven empires. It is also stated that five of these empires have fallen or were in a previous time. Which empires are being referred to in this text? The five are **Egyptian, Assyrian, Babylonian, Persian, and Greek** Empires. The one which existed during the period of the writing of the book of Revelation is the **Roman** Empire. The first difference between the book of Revelation, and what one learns from Daniel, is that the vision from the book of Revelation begins looking at the world's empires earlier. Two additional empires which persecuted the Jewish people are included, Egypt and Assyria. If we allow for this, then Rome would be the fourth, as it is in Daniel's dream. When considering Nebuchadnezzar's dream, one must remember the relationship between the fourth empire and the fifth; both have iron. It was previously stated that this repetition of the same material teaches that one should expect a reappearing of the Roman Empire in the last days. In regard to this, John, the author of the book of Revelation, says that this empire must remain only a short while. As one continues to read in Revelation, he learns that this seventh empire, although short-lived in comparison with the others, will return again, for a third time.

"And the beast which was and is not also he is the eighth; and he is from the seventh, and into destruction he goes away." Revelation 17:11

At first glance this may seem confusing, but one must remember that he is reading apocalyptic literature which often times is written in a unique manner in order to reveal a greater amount of information. Numbers are important and contain a symbolic meaning. It has already been discussed that the number four has a global quality to it. Hence, Daniel's dream spoke about kingdoms that rule over most of the earth. Whereas Nebuchadnezzar's dream spoke of five empires, the idea that the number five conveys is that which is insufficient or incomplete...something that does not fulfill its objective. In other words, Nebuchadnezzar's dream of this image is a composite of world empires that would not endure nor fulfill its desire to champion over the rule of G-d. The fifth one would be divided among itself and be broken only to give rise to the Kingdom of G-d (See Daniel 2:41-45).

When one examines John's vision in Revelation chapter 17, he sees what relates to the first seven empires. Why seven? Because the number seven refers to sanctification; in other words, G-d has set apart seven empires in His plan which will ultimately bring about the establishment of His Kingdom. The reader is then told that the seventh is also the eighth. The number eight relates to that which is new. It is also related to the concepts of redemption and the kingdom. Hence, it will be with the destruction of the eighth empire that the Kingdom of G-d will be established.

Also discussed in this chapter are the ten horns.

"And the ten horns which you saw, they are ten kings which a kingdom not yet have they received; but authority as kings for one hour they receive with the beast. They have one mindset, and their power and authority to the beast they shall give." Revelation 17:12-13

Once again the similarities between the book of Revelation and Daniel are clearly seen. Both books agree that the ten horns represent ten kings. There is also an agreement that the ten kings will be manifested in the final empire (beast) which will war against the purposes and the followers of the One True G-d. Previously it was pointed out that the Roman Empire will surface three times (The sixth, seventh, and eighth empires). Obviously the first occurred over two thousand years ago, from 27 BC until 476 AD. In regard to the second occurrence, one must make a decision. One must accept that either the great persecution of Jews during Hitler's Third Reich meets the criteria for being considered as a "Roman Empire", or expect that prior to the final beast, there will be another short-lived attempt to rule the world that will meet the parameters of those (**Egypt, Assyria, Babylon, Persia, Greece, and Rome**) which came before it. What did all of these empires have in common? The answer is that the Jewish people suffered under these empires.

It must be pointed out that the capital of these empires varied in location; however, these empires shared much of the same land. In other words, these empires varied in the ethnicity and nationality of its leaders but not so much in the area over which the empire ruled. Some have pointed out that the Persian Empire did not persecute the Jewish people nearly to the extent of the others. In fact, it was Cyrus who allowed many of the Jews to return to Israel and rebuild the Temple. Other Persian kings also assisted the Jewish people, such as Darius and Artaxerxes; yet one only needs to read Nehemiah's response to the condition of Jerusalem in chapters one and two of the book that bears his name, or the story of Esther, to know that life during the administration of the Medes and Persians were often very difficult for the Jewish people.

Nazi Germany and the Roman Empire

Certainly the Holocaust represents the greatest persecution of Jewish people that has occurred in history. It is for this reason that it is hard to believe that the Scriptures would be silent on this issue. Perhaps they are not. In studying the beast from Revelation chapter 17, the sixth empire (head) mentioned was Rome. This empire is said to reappear for a short time and is also the eighth. Is one to conclude that the barbaric rule of Adolph Hitler's Nazis, which were responsible for over 6 million Jewish deaths and 50 million deaths (some estimates are as high as 70 million) that occurred in total during WWII, or nearly four percent of the world's population at the time, is the seventh empire? If so, then the Nazi Empire would be the seventh. Such a view is not new, as others have suggested it. For this was a primary argument in Robert Van Kampen's book "The Sign".

"Van Kampen's idea of a new revival of a Third Reich is noteworthy, particularly with the Islamic obsession with Hitler's book 'Mein Kaumpf' which Muslims translated as 'Jihad'. Van Kampen's timing of his writing did not give him all the information we have today on radical Islam. Therefore his

assessment of a revived Third Reich, I believe is ingenious..."
(From a soon to be publish work entitled "Musterion" by Sergio F.
Cabrera)

Earlier on in the book of Revelation, this same issue of the
empires is addressed. In chapter 13, John receives a vision of a
beast coming out of the sea. In this vision John sees the beast in
the opposite order to that of Daniel. Whereas Daniel's order of
the beast was the lion, bear and leopard; John saw the leopard
first and then the bear and lion. John also informs the reader that
it is Satan who gave them their power and authority. Even though
seven heads are mentioned, it would seem that ultimately this
vision is of only one empire. The passage tells the reader that the
empire is like a leopard. Leopards are opportunists, having a wide
range of prey. Their hunting techniques are among the best in the
jungle, quietly drawing near to their target and pouncing on their
victim, who did not realize the danger in which he was in until he
felt the sting of death. Leopards always dominate their prey.
Whereas the beast is said to be like a leopard, he is said to have
feet like a bear. The feet of a bear are his foundation, they are
long and upon them he rises when fighting. Finally, this beast is
said to have a mouth like a lion. A lion's roar is loud and is most
intimidating. It is said concerning this beast that he speaks great
blasphemies against the L-rd. It may be this characteristic that is
the reason it is said that the mouth of the beast is like a lion.

An interesting perspective which some have offered in regard to
understanding this vision is that the seventh beast will be a
composite of the worst characteristics of the empires which
preceded it. It is also said to continue for a short while and then
suffers a fatal blow which later is healed to the amazement of the
world (See Revelation 13:3). The passage describes a feeling of
futility in regard to fighting against this beast. It is clear that this
empire is utterly against all which is related to the Living G-d.

*"And he opened his mouth in blasphemies against G-d, to
blaspheme His Name and His Sanctuary. And it was given to him
to make war with the saints and to overcome them; and it was*

given to him authority over every tribe and language and nation."
Revelation 13:6-7

This empire will no doubt be cruel and demand absolute submissiveness. Masses will pledge loyalty out of fear and a sense of hopelessness. Whether or not this empire will actually utilize the symbols and the name Nazi is not the primary issue. This prophecy reveals that an empire based in Europe, with its heritage rooted in that of the ancient Greek and Roman Empires will resurface in the end times. While most suggest that the Third Reich was a designation which properly refers to the later Medieval Roman Empire and the Modern German Empire, I would offer an alternate possibility. Hitler called his Nazi regime the Third Reich because he himself saw it as a rebirth of ancient Greek and Roman Empires. Hitler believed that the Arian race was divinely endowed with superior traits and capabilities. The Arians had their historical origins with the Greeks and Latin (Roman) people. Proper study of Hitler reveals an obsession with the likes of Alexander the Great and the Roman emperors. Accounts of his passion for artifacts and relics of these periods are also well documented.

What is the relationship between this final empire and Islam? The answer to this question is revealed in Daniel chapter 8.

The Goat from the West

Nearly all interpreters of this chapter see it as relating to the past. Such a view, however, is in contrast to some of the internal evidence of the text itself. Twice in this passage the reader is told that the events of this chapter relate to the end times (See verses 17 and 19). Daniel received this prophecy in the third year of King Belshazzar. Belshazzar, the grandson of Nebuchadnezzar, ascended to throne after his father's reign of twenty-three years. It is interesting that after discussing King Darius the Mede (the Persian Empire) in chapter 6 that the narrative returns to an earlier time, the Babylonian period.

The vision in chapter 8 is related to the visions of chapters 2 and 7. It is also of great significance that while Belshazzar was a Babylonian king, Daniel is said to be in Shushan, the capital of the Persian Empire. It is very clear from this vision that Persia, modern day Iran, is being emphasized in this eighth chapter. The first portion of this vision is of a ram which has two horns. The text informs the reader that one horn is higher than the other. According to the commentators, the horns represent leaders or kings. Hence, it is the second king of this empire who obtains a greater prominence and expands his empire. Not only is he able to expand his rule, he does so with ease and without any real resistance, as there were none who were able to mount any meaningful opposition to him. Although this empire is situated in the east, modern Iran, he expands his rule towards the west, north, and south.

"I saw the ram goring towards the west and north and south and all the beasts (other nations) *were not able to stand before him and there was no deliverer from his hand; and he did according to what he wanted and he became great."*
Daniel 8:4

It is clear that this empire is out of the east and although it is expanding north and south, the primary direction of its rule is westward. It is during this expansion that suddenly the reader is informed that a goat burst on the scene. This goat is said to cross the surface of the earth without touching it (See verse five). This description may be implying some supernatural ability. This ability is not from G-d, for later on it will be demonstrated that this one opposes the things of G-d and therefore this special endowment of power is from Satan. The goat is said to have a unique horn between its eyes and he fights and defeats the ram, breaking off its two horns.

It is this unique horn of the goat that is eventually broken off and the appearance of four others that will come up underneath it, moving in the direction of the four winds. As has been stated previously, four represents a global aspect; therefore, it is from the west that a final empire will arise and rule the world. The text continues and states that from this empire will appear a "little horn". This "little horn" represents a wicked leader who expands his kingdom towards the south and the east in order to arrive at the promise land— Israel. This empire not only wars with those of this world, but the Scripture states,

> "*It was exalted to the host of heaven and fell towards the earth; from the host and the stars and he trampled them. And unto the prince of the host he exalted himself and because of him the daily offering was removed and the foundation of his sanctuary was cast down.*" Daniel 8:10-11

The information provided in this section makes it clear that this prophecy deals with the end times. The battle that is described is highly spiritual and represents the conflict between Satan and a heavenly prince who will ultimately bring about the Kingdom of G-d. This battle will be discussed in greater detail later on. The final section of this chapter offers an explanation of this prophecy. It is most significant that it is Gabriel who is sent to offer this explanation to Daniel. Gabriel is the angel who, according to Jewish tradition, is connected to the final redemption. Therefore it should not surprise the students of the New Testament that it was him who announced the birth of Yeshua. In Gabriel's explanation to Daniel, he states that the ram and its two horns represent the kings of the Medes and Persians. Once again, it must be stressed that Gabriel clearly reveals that this vision concerns the end times and not the time of the ancient Persian Empire.

The goat that is mentioned, which defeats the ram, is the king of Greece. In a similar way that the Greek Empire emerged under Alexander the Great and defeated the Persians, so too, in the last days, will a similar occurrence take place. This will provide an historical backdrop to assist the reader, and those who will witness such events, to understand what is happening. It must be pointed out that although the word "Greece" is used, the idea which is being conveyed here is that of a European Empire.

Before moving on with a fuller discussion of these events, it would be helpful to connect some of the things discussed in the previous chapters with this vision from Daniel.

Daniel Chapter 8 and Today...

If one believes that he is living near the beginning of the last days, and considers what Daniel chapter 8 is saying, it would not be hard to imagine the intent of this vision in light of current events. The Middle Eastern nation that is growing in power and prominence today, having greater influence than any other, is Iran. Iran has formed strong relations with Turkey and Syria. Iran also wields enormous power in Lebanon, by means of Hezbollah. Iran has strengthened her relationship with North Korea, Russia, and other nations. Iran's desire to destroy Israel is well known, as she assists in numerous ways terrorist organizations like Hamas in their efforts to undermine Israel's security. Iran's government is highly Islamic and it is clear that she has played a role in destabilizing administrations of Middle Eastern nations whose leaders do not share her Islamic view.

As Islam moves into the West, Iran is gaining more influence and support from many of the Muslims that populate Europe and North America. As stated previously, Islam is a violent religion which has demonstrated time and time again its willingness to use barbaric practices to achieve its goals. At the time of this writing, the world's most well-known Islamic terrorist was captured and killed in Pakistan. The events surrounding the killing of Osama bin Laden shed great light on the place of Islam throughout much of the Middle East. When the reports of bin Laden's death and the details were revealed, it became clear that the Pakistani government was willfully assisting him. How else could it be explained that such a wanted individual could live in a military city, in a large compound, without attracting the curiosity of government officials in a country which is well known as a police state. It is unimaginable that a home so significantly larger than the others in the neighborhood, with the security features that it had, would not cause Pakistani intelligence officials to inquire in regard to its residents. Who was the owner, who built it, how the compound was paid for, are just a few of the questions that the government would have certainly asked and worked to have answered. The fact that it was only a kilometer from the main Pakistani military academy would only serve to have heightened the interest of the Pakistani intelligence agency.

Even if one accepts the highly improbable claims of the Pakistani government that they did not know that Osama bin Laden was located in that compound, it is impossible to defend their harsh and offensive response to the United States after the world was informed concerning the killing of bin Laden. One would think the Pakistani government would have expressed gratitude to America for capturing and killing such a dangerous fugitive who could have carried out terrorist acts against Pakistan, since supposedly the government was aiding in the fight against terror and providing intelligence concerning bin Laden's Al-Qaida terror organization. However, rather than thanking the United States, the former Pakistani President Pervez Musharraf lashed out at America for violating its sovereignty and threatened a military response against the American military forces if other attacks against terrorists are made in Pakistan.

Some in the Obama administration have said that such statements are made not out of sincerity, but for internal consumption by the Pakistani people. Although I strongly disagree, even if this were true, then it shows the strong position that Islam holds in a country like Pakistan. If most Muslims are good, peace loving people and only a small minority is radical, then why is there a need to make such statements, since only a small fraction of the Pakistani Muslims would be displeased with the American action? When one considers all the facts objectively, the most reasonable conclusion is that true Islam is radical and violent and holds an ever-growing position in the Middle East and Asia. This growth and sphere of influence is spreading rapidly in Europe and North America and ought to be of great concern to all.

Islam is not the religion of the beast, rather it will be the beast that will move against Islam and destroy it and all other religions that do not embrace the primary tenets of this final empire's "religion". The beast, which is the final empire, and the "little horn", who is its leader, will rise out of Europe and establish a rule that will comprise the world. It is this leader, likened in the vision to a "little horn", that is described in the New Testament as the Antichrist. It is the Antichrist and how he rises to power and the events surrounding this, which will be the subject of the next chapter.

Chapter 6

"The Antichrist"

When one examines in the Scriptures the term "Antichrist", he will find that it is used in two distinct, but related manners. The first is obviously for the one who will arise in the end times and rule over a world empire that opposes and persecutes the things and the people of G-d. This is the most common usage. The second use has to do with a type of spirit that is false and denies that Yeshua is the Messiah and that He is from G-d.

> *"And every spirit which does not confess Messiah Yeshua in the flesh has come, is not from G-d. And this one is the antichrist..."* I John 4:3

This verse, along with a few other verses, makes it clear that those who deny the divinity of Yeshua will unite with the Antichrist and join his effort to thwart the plans and purposes of the Living G-d. The point which must be grasped is that it is not so much what the Antichrist is for, but rather what he is against that defines him, namely the Person (identity) and work of Messiah Yeshua. Therefore, it is not so much that people initially must be for him; rather simply they are against the Biblical Yeshua.

Today, several individuals, such as Joel Richardson and Walid Shoebat, have written that it is Islam which will be the religion of the Antichrist. However, such a perspective is difficult to reconcile with the vision of Daniel chapter 8. As Islam spreads and exerts its oppressive laws on others, conflicts will emerge and the battle between the goat and the ram will be realized when the people of the West will wage war against the expansion of Islam westward. The Western empire, based in Europe, will also move at first to defend Israel against Islam's desire to exterminate the Nation of Israel and the Jewish people. Although both Israel and the Jewish people in general will suffer greatly, this period of persecution is not what the prophet Jeremiah foretold in Jeremiah 30 and verse 7.

Prior to the time of which Jeremiah spoke, Israel will be attacked by a confederacy of Islamic nations, led by Iran. This war will be the means by which a forced peace agreement between Israel and her neighbors will come about. It will be the West (Goat) who, after defeating the East (Ram), will allow Israel to return to her ancient religious practice, including a sacrificial service. It is this return to sacrificial worship which is the key prophetic sign. In Daniel chapter nine, an agreement is discussed. The word used is actually "covenant". It will be a covenant which will allow Israel to offer sacrifices. The text from chapter nine makes it very clear that it is the Antichrist who will establish this covenant (See Daniel 9:27). Why would the Antichrist want to defend Israel and allow them the right to build an altar and resume their ancient practices?

Most believe that because the Antichrist is against the things of G-d, he would never be part of something that would benefit Israel and the Jewish people or the religion of Judaism. The error of many is in not realizing that the L-rd's primary desire is to establish His Kingdom. Because Israel will play a major role in this coming about, the Antichrist will at first do kind acts toward Israel and the Jewish people in an attempt to court them away from G-d and obeying His will. The text is clear that after seemingly supporting Israel, he will, in the middle of the seven year peace agreement, annul it and remove the daily sacrifice. This event, called the Abomination of Desolation, will be discussed in a later chapter. The point one must glean here is that after defeating Islam, the West will take certain measures to ensure that such religious extremism does not resurface in the future. This is one of the implications of Daniel 7:25 which informs the reader that the Antichrist will change laws.

The West, under the eventual leadership of the Antichrist, will move to establish a set of parameters to which all religious expressions must submit. One of the chief tenets will be religious pluralism. Any religious expression claiming to be the truth and relevant for all individuals, will be strongly opposed by this Western Empire. Such a religion will be viewed as narrow-minded, intolerant, and proclaiming a self-superiority that will be seen as violating the chief tenet of religious pluralism. Hence, Yeshua's claims to be the only Begotten of the Father, and that only through Him is one saved and thereby able to enter into a relationship with the True G-d, will be ruled not only offensive, but unacceptable in this empire and therefore outlawed. One can be a "Christian" in this empire, but not the type of Christian (a real one) who relies on the authority of the Scriptural texts for his beliefs. This will cause those who believe such compromises empty Christianity from its basic tenets, to be persecuted. This tribulation will also be discussed in greater detail in a later chapter.

In returning to the primary subject of this section, which is that the Antichrist will speak great things, i.e., blasphemies, one learns that he will be empowered by Satan. It will be by Satan's influence that the Antichrist will be able to do many supernatural signs and gain leadership of this Western Empire.

> *"And all authority of the first beast he* (the Antichrist) *exercises before him* (the beast). *And he makes the earth and all who dwell in it that they should worship the first beast which had healed his wound of death. And he does great signs in order that he should make fire to come down from the heavens on the earth before mankind. And he deceives the ones dwelling upon the earth by means of these signs which were given to him to do before the beast..."*
> Revelation 13:12-14a

Daniel's description is very similar to that of the book of Revelation as John also prophesied,

> *"And in the end of their empire...a boldface king will stand who understands enigmas. The strength of his power is not his power and in wonders he will destroy and will prosper*

and will do and will destroy mighty ones and the holy people. And concerning his intelligence he will succeed, his power is deception and in it he will grow conceited and in "peace" destroy many..." Daniel 8:23-25a

Several important pieces of information are contained in this passage. Once again, the Antichrist is described as possessing a supernatural power which is not his own. He will use this power not only to do mighty acts, but to deceive. His promises of peace will be broken and in actuality he will kill many. Ultimately, he will set himself against the people of G-d. These things will take place in a very specific order. It is imperative for the reader to recognize these events in their proper sequence in order to correctly interpret these events which the Scripture foretells.

Although the Antichrist will present himself as a wise solver of problems and initially demonstrate this, in the end he will bring great suffering and misery on the world. He will promise peace and deliver it, but only to further his plans of world domination and self-exaltation. In spite of all the hope the people will place in him, tribulation is what he ultimately will bring upon the world.

Tribulation and the Antichrist

Tribulation is a theme which characterizes the end times. In studying tribulation in the Bible one must always be aware of the source of the tribulation. Failure to do so has caused great problems when interpreting the prophecies concerning the events of the last days. The issue here is whether G-d is the source of the tribulation or Satan. The Bible makes it very clear *that believers in Messiah Yeshua will not go through the tribulation which is from G-d.* Such tribulation is known as the wrath of G-d. The Apostle Paul writes in regard to the wrath of G-d,

> *"For G-d has not appointed us for wrath, rather for obtaining salvation by means of our L-rd Messiah Yeshua."*
>
> I Thessalonians 5:9

It has previously been stated that the Antichrist will make an agreement (covenant) allowing Israel to return to her sacrificial services. This agreement will be for seven years. In addition to Israel offering sacrifices, many other events will be taking place during this time. Many people erroneously believe that during the entire seven years G-d will be pouring out His wrath. This is not the case. In fact, it is impossible to prove such a position through the Scriptures. It has also been previously stated that in the middle of the seven years, the Antichrist will terminate this agreement. Hence, this seven year period can be broken into two periods. Next, a discussion of the events which will take place during the first half will be presented.

In chapter one, the first four seals of Revelation chapter six were studied. There was a clear relationship between these seals and the first section of Matthew chapter 24. Messiah Yeshua, when speaking about these events, called them the beginning of sorrows (See Matthew 24:8). Whether these events are in the seven year period or precede this time is impossible to know with certainty. Perhaps a few of these happenings are and others are not. However, when arriving at the fifth seal and what is described in Matthew 24:9-14, one can be certain that this persecution of believers which will take place in the last days is an event that takes place during the first half of the seven years. The reason one can be sure about this is that the persecution of believers ends with an event known as the Abomination of Desolation. A fuller discussion of the Abomination of Desolation, and why this event brings an end to the persecution of believers, will be studied later. The focus of this present section is the similarities between Matthew 24:9-14 and Revelation 6:9-17.

Matthew 24:9-14

After Yeshua finishes speaking about the wars, conflicts, earthquakes, famines, and pestilence, He then summarizes these things by stating that these are only the beginning. He then begins speaking about how His followers will be delivered up to both intense affliction and even to death. When speaking about believers, Yeshua uses the second person plural to denote them. It is important to note that those persecuting them are all the nations. In other words, the entire world will be strongly opposed to Messiah's followers during this period. In fact, the text actually says that all the nations will hate believers because of our connection to the Name of Yeshua. This statement may be implying something somewhat different than might appear at first reading. It may not be the name Yeshua that brings the persecution, but one needs to remember that in the Scripture the term "name" is synonymous with character. Hence, the people who will be hated and receiving persecution are not those who simply identify themselves as Christian, but rather those who truly live out the teachings of Messiah as revealed in the Word of G-d and thereby develop a character which is like His.

In this same section the word "betray" appears. This term reveals that the authority which will be ruling during this period will seek to arrest believers. Elsewhere in the Bible the reader is told that family members, friends, and even those who profess faith, but in actuality have none, will turn true believers over to the government (See Mark 13:12 and Luke 21:12-17). During this period, numerous false prophets and teachers will capture the attention of many and through their false words many will be deceived. Sin and lawlessness will abound. It is important to understand that during this time of immorality, it is the laws of G-d which are being violated, not necessarily civil law.

It is vital for one to remember that it is the previous section which dealt with the wars, conflicts, earthquakes, famines, and pestilence that will bring about chaos in the world and cause the masses to cry out for change. It is in response to this cry for change that a world government will be established. This new government will be the final beast, i.e. empire, that will arise and from which the Antichrist will rule. This empire will, in the short term, bring about peace and economic prosperity and even appear to solve the problems in the Middle East. Although from a secular perspective things will be greatly improved, the spiritual condition of the world will decay. It will be the believers who oppose the ungodliness of this new empire who will become a target of intense persecution. Not only will believers be speaking out against the gross violations of the Word of G-d which will characterize this empire, but they will also be proclaiming the Gospel message (See Matthew 24:14). It is these two acts by believers that will cause their time of tribulation.

When examining the behavior that brings about this tribulation upon the followers of Messiah, it becomes most clear that G-d could not be the source of this tribulation. Rather it is, of course, Satan who hates it when individuals obey the Word of G-d and honor Yeshua.

Revelation 6:9-17

When examining this section of Revelation chapter six, there are obvious connections with Yeshua's teachings in Matthew chapter 24. When the fifth seal is opened, John sees under the altar the souls of those who were killed for two reasons. The first is their obedience to the Word of G-d and the second is their faithful testimony. It is clear that these individuals did indeed live in such a way as to bear witness concerning their L-rd, Messiah Yeshua. Those who were slain were crying out to the L-rd with a very specific request,

> "And they cried out with a loud voice saying, 'Until when O L-rd Holy and True, do You not judge and avenge our blood from those who dwell upon the earth?" Revelation 6:10

This statement makes it clear that the wrath of G-d had not yet begun. It is only when one arrives at the sixth seal that the issue of the wrath of G-d begins to be addressed. In the 12th verse two important clues are given to the reader. He learns that when the sixth seal is opened, among the events that take place are that the sun becomes black as sackcloth and the moon becomes red as blood. This information is parallel to what one reads in the prophecy of Joel,

"The sun was turned to darkness and the moon to blood before the coming of the great and awesome Day of the L-rd." Joel 3:4 (Joel 2:31 in English translations)

It is from the context of the prophecy of Joel that once again it is clear that G-d's wrath is very imminent, but is not the source of the events of any of the previous seals. The reason why G-d's wrath is alluded to in the sixth seal is to call people to repentance. The fact that the sun is described as having a likeness of sackcloth is also a hint to repentance, as sackcloth was worn in Biblical times in order to convey both mourning and a repentant heart. The changes that occurred with the sun and moon, along with other cosmic changes that are described in this sixth seal, all share one purpose. This purpose is to capture the attention of the people and demonstrate that G-d is moving in a unique way. It is clear from the response of the people that they understand that G-d's judgment is approaching. Unfortunately, instead of turning towards G-d in repentance, the people simply want to hide. It is clear from the following two verses that the people are indeed aware of the L-rd's displeasure with them and that Messiah died for them sacrificially, yet they sadly do not want any connection with G-d nor His Messiah.

"And they said to the mountains and to the rocks, 'Fall upon us and hide us from the face of Him that sits upon the throne and from the wrath of the Lamb; for has come the great day of His wrath and who is able to stand.'" Revelation 6:16-17

Even though it appears from verse 17 that the wrath of G-d has come, the Greek use of the past tense in this instance is simply to emphasize the nearness of G-d's judgment. For it becomes most clear from chapter seven that the angels who have been given the assignment to pour out the L-rd's wrath are not allowed to do so until the servants of G-d were sealed (See Revelation 7:3). Chapter seven also reveals that there is an inherent relationship between these servants and Israel.

Now that it has been demonstrated that believers will suffer intense tribulation and that this persecution will be part of the opposition of the Antichrist to the purposes of G-d, it shall now be presented how these events are related to one another. In short, because believers will be the only opposition to the Antichrist, he will act to remove them from the face of the earth. He will characterize them as religious fanatics who pose the same danger that Islam did. It will be through this objective to rid the world of believers that a network of intelligence gathering will be put into place which the Antichrist will use not only against believers, but all whom he believes are a threat to his rule. In other words, a Gestapo-like entity, similar to what Hitler created, will be incorporated into this empire. The greatest tool this new "Gestapo" will utilize is revealed also in the book of Revelation.

It has already been discussed that the Antichrist will possess great intelligence and that he will use this in order to deceive people. He will do miracles to capture the attention and admiration of the world. Once achieving this, he will command those in his empire to make an image to the beast, i.e. empire. There are several reasons why the Antichrist would order all people to make such an image. First, one must understand that the word used in this passage (Revelation 13:14-15) for image denotes an object of worship. It is very important to comprehend what is said by John in this section.

> "*And it was given to him to grant spirit* (life) *to the image of the beast, in order that he should speak and should make those who do not worship the image of the beast to be killed.*" Revelation 13:15

From this verse it becomes evident that this empire is not at all secular in nature. The empire and its leader, which are empowered and guided by Satan, seek worship. Although this empire was initially defined by its foundational tenet of religious pluralism, once in power, there is a quick and abrupt change. Satan always coveted the worship that the True G-d received and he has always been about usurping the authority of the L-rd and to establish his kingdom in place of the True Kingdom of the Living G-d. The obsession of being worshipped is seen in the fact that if anyone refuses to worship the beast, this one will be killed. Now it is possible to rightly understand this image as a monitoring system which will reveal to this new "Gestapo" who is not absolutely loyal to the empire.

One must ask the question, who would refuse not only to worship the beast, but even to make the image? The answer is those who take seriously the Word of G-d, as it is clearly forbidden in the Ten Commandments to behave in such a manner. The empire will want to identify any who might oppose it. Not only will the image be used to identify those who are loyal to it, but additionally, one reads in the final few verses of this chapter that in order to engage in any form of commerce one will be required to receive a mark either on his right hand or upon his forehead. Over the years much has been made concerning this mark. Many individuals have offered numerous suggestions, most of which border on the absurd. The only point that I will offer is that the mark of the beast is not something that one is going to receive by mistake. That is, a person will not receive it without knowing what he is doing. The empire will want to make it most clear to all its demand for absolute loyalty. It would defeat the purpose if people received the mark and did not understand the pledge they were in fact making to the empire. Due to everyone's need to buy and sell, failure to receive the mark would make it virtually impossible to exist.

People who refuse to make the image or receive the mark will have to work together. Both true believers and followers of Torah-based Judaism will be brought together, as both of these groups will refuse to comply with these demands. With the identifying of the opponents of the empire, an intense time of persecution will begin. Most people will not care or oppose the killing of believers or observant Jews. They will be seen as religious fundamentalists and their beliefs pose a threat to the peace and prosperity which has been created by the empire. Most of the Jewish community will have embraced this empire and its leader. After all, he delivered Israel from her Islamic neighbors and even allowed Judaism to return to its historical form, granting an altar and either a tabernacle or perhaps even the Temple to be rebuilt. However, when most of the believers have been killed along with the small percentage of observant Jews who comprise the Jewish community, there will be a significant change in the character of the empire.

The initial religious diversity reflected by one of the major tenets of the beast (this empire) has already been altered when worship of the beast was demanded from all people. This change will be followed by a declaration which ultimately will reveal its true intention. Because Satan will be empowering this empire and the Antichrist is a type of Satan incarnate, eventually the Antichrist will demand that he be worshipped. This now sets the stage for one of the most significant events that will take place in human history.

The Abomination of Desolation

The first mention of this event occurs in Daniel 9:26-27. In this passage, all that can be determined is that this event will bring about a cessation of the sacrifices which were reinstituted by means of the covenant established by the Antichrist. Also in Matthew 24, the Abomination of Desolation is mentioned. The context for this reference is very informative. One must remember that in this chapter Yeshua speaks about the initial troubles which will take place throughout the world. There will be economic, political, and natural disturbances which will bring about utter chaos in the world. These occurrences will give rise to instability and eventually a world organization will be created to deal with these problems. As a result, a new world government will be established from which the Antichrist will arise and assume control. After the conclusion of what Yeshua called the "beginning of sorrows", a period of persecution of believers will begin. One needs to remember that in discussing this persecution, Yeshua spoke about His followers in the second person— "you". This section ended with the statement that the Gospel message will be preached throughout the world and then the end shall come (See Matthew 24:14). To what "end" is this verse referring?

Immediately after mentioning the "end" the reader encounters this verse, where Messiah reveals,

"Therefore whenever you should see the Abomination of Desolation, that which was spoken of by the Prophet Daniel, standing in the Holy Place (the one who is reading let him understand) then let those in Judea flee unto the mountains."

Matthew 24:15-16

It is informative that after speaking of the Abomination of Desolation there is a significant grammatical change. Yeshua changes from using the second person "you" to the third person "let him". In other words, He changes from speaking about believers who were being persecuted, to those residing in Judea (Israel), instructing them to flee to the mountains. Why does He make this change? In order to find the answer one must examine another citation concerning the Abomination of Desolation. In this occurrence, Paul is speaking to believers who are discussing the last days and Yeshua's promise of gathering up believers and taking them into the heavens, i.e. the Rapture. It is from this passage that the student of the Bible learns what exactly the Abomination of Desolation is. Paul writes,

"Do not allow any man to deceive you in any manner, because unless first shall come the apostasy and be revealed the man of sin—the son of destruction; the one who opposes and exalts himself above all that is called G-d and is worshiped; with the result that in the sanctuary of G-d as G-d he sits manifesting himself that he is G-d."

II Thessalonians 2:3-4

Hence, the Abomination of Desolation is when the Antichrist puts an end to the daily sacrifices in Jerusalem and enters into the sanctuary and states that he is G-d. Paul states in this passage that the Rapture will not happen until after this event takes place. For this was the question that the believers in Thessalonica were asking Paul and to which he said that first the Abomination of Desolation must occur. What does Paul's statement mean for the doctrine of "imminency"? This question and others relating to the Rapture will be the subject of the next chapter. The issue at hand is twofold. First, what does the Abomination of Desolation have to do with the "end" which was mentioned in Matthew 24:14 and how does this event relate to the Jewish people?

If in fact the Abomination of Desolation is an event which believers will witness and because the context for Paul's statement in Second Thessalonians chapter 2 was the Rapture, then the "end" that Messiah is addressing is the end of the "Church age". With believers being removed from earth, the focus of the Antichrist will be Israel. Up until the Abomination of Desolation, the majority of Jewish people will have supported the empire and the leadership of the Antichrist, as they did not know his true identity or his ultimate purpose. However when the Antichrist shall enter into the sanctuary and proclaim himself to be G-d, Israel will overwhelmingly reject him. What will their rejection bring about? The answer is found in the prophecy of Jeremiah chapter 30. There, one reads about a period of time when Israel will suffer intense persecution, known as "Jacob's Trouble". It is vital for one to remember that Jacob's Trouble comes after the Abomination of Desolation, in the second half of the seven year agreement (covenant) that one reads about in the latter portion of Daniel chapter 9.

This period of tribulation and the events surrounding it will be the focus of a later chapter.

Chapter 7

"The Rapture"

Although the Rapture was mentioned in the previous chapter, we have not yet defined nor examined it thoroughly, according to the Scripture. This will be the subject of this section. There are not many references to the Rapture in the Bible; however, when looking at the two primary texts which discuss the Rapture, it becomes clear that it is a reality and not based upon speculation nor is it a man made doctrine. The first passage that will be examined is found in I Thessalonians chapter four. Towards the end of this chapter, Paul comments about those who have died as believers in Messiah Yeshua. One of the primary themes in this section is hope. To what hope is Paul referring? In another passage, which contains an additional reference to the Rapture (I Corinthians 15), Paul speaks about a new and glorified body which believers will receive at Messiah's return. This body is designed for heaven and the holiness characterized by the Kingdom of G-d. It is this new body which is the hope that each believer has and will provide the encouragement to remain steadfast in difficult times.

It causes much confusion when one does not make a distinction between when Messiah returns to gather up believers (both those living and those who are dead) to heaven, i.e. the Rapture, and when Messiah returns to establish His Kingdom—The Second Coming. **These are two separate events**. When Paul speaks of hope in the I Thessalonians passage, the hope to which he is referring is the new body. The believers in Thessalonica knew of this hope, but thought those who died prior to Messiah's return would miss out on receiving this glorified body as they, i.e. their souls, were already with Messiah in the heavens. It is this concern Paul is addressing. In speaking about this concern, he writes that in the same way one believes that Messiah Yeshua died and rose again, so too will those who died in Messiah rise (See I Thessalonians 4:14). It is not a coincidence that Paul inserts into this discussion the concept of the resurrection.

The Rapture is likened to a resurrection by Paul also in First Corinthians chapter 15. In speaking about the Rapture, he uses the term "mystery". Some have pointed out that this term is used because the Rapture was not a doctrine known or spoken about by the Jewish sages. When referring to the dead, Paul shows a tendency to speak of them as merely sleeping. This was a common occurrence in Judaism, as the primary prayer in all major Jewish prayer services, called the "Amidah", speaks of the dead "as those sleeping in their graves". The rabbinical sages point out that this use of the term "sleeping" as a reference to the dead, points to a sure hope that death is not the end, nor does death separate one from the promises of G-d, no more than one who is sleeping is cut off from the world.

To the Corinthians, Paul likens the Rapture to the resurrection of the Messiah, so that they would understand that just as the resurrection is foundational to our faith, so too is the Rapture. Paul states in chapter 15 that, without the resurrection, the foundation of the Christian faith in Yeshua is without merit.

"But if Messiah had not been raised, cursed is our preaching and empty is your faith." I Corinthian 15:14

Paul twice (verses 20 and 23) refers to the resurrected Messiah as the "Firstfruits". This term would have great significance to a Jewish individual. Jewish people were part of the Corinthian community, as an inscription identifying a synagogue has been found there. The term "Firstfruits" is a reference to a special service which took place on the first Sunday after the first day of the festival of Unleavened Bread (See Leviticus 23:9-14). Few Christians realize that Paul calls the resurrected Yeshua by this title so as to teach the believer about a wonderful hope he possesses. One needs to remember that a fifty day harvest period began with the day of the Firstfruits. On the very day Messiah rose from the dead, Jewish individuals would bring the first portion of their harvest to the Priest (the Levitical priesthood) and make a prayer that the rest of the harvest would be like the Firstfruits. In the L-rd's providence, Yeshua not only was crucified on Passover, but was resurrected on the day of Firstfruits as a Scriptural way of promising believers that we, "the rest of the harvest", will be like the Firstfruits—Yeshua!

With this knowledge it is much easier to comprehend the significance of Paul's statement to both the Thessalonians and the Corinthians concerning the Rapture. He is stating that all believers, whether alive or dead, shall be changed (See I Corinthians 15:51-57). The change that all believers can expect to receive at the Rapture is to be transformed into a new glorified body which will reflect the very character of Messiah Yeshua. In other words, believers will be like Him—not of course divine, but reflecting the godliness and holiness of the Living G-d, the original purpose that the L-rd created man to demonstrate.

Although no man knows the time of the Rapture, one can discern from the Bible that the Rapture occurs soon after the Abomination of Desolation. Some find this statement to violate the doctrine of imminency. This doctrine states that the return of the Messiah to gather up believers may occur at any time. Those who hold to this doctrine believe that there are no events remaining today which must take place prior to the Rapture. The Scriptural basis for this doctrine is found in a few verses.

> *"But concerning that day and hour, no one knows; not even the angels in heaven, except My Father only."*
> Matthew 24:36

> *"On account this also you be ready, because at the hour you do not think the Son of man comes."* Matthew 24:44

Although there are a few additional verses which could be included, all Scripture relating to the doctrine of imminency have a common theme—man does not know the time of Messiah's return. Because this doctrine is reasoned by means of Scripture, and it is not directly stated in a verse that Messiah's return is imminent, it would be helpful to apply some rules of logic to this issue. It is illogical for one to conclude that because something is unknown, it may happen at any time. Those who hold to this doctrine hold fast to imminency for the Rapture, but not for the Second Coming of Messiah, even though no one knows the time for the Second Coming either. Such individuals rightly claim that the Bible reveals events which must precede the Second Coming, but err in believing that no such events exist prior to the Rapture. What should one do with the verses which state clearly that believers will suffer satanic persecution? Obviously one could argue that throughout the last 2,000 years believers have suffered persecution from Satan. This is true; however Messiah states in the Matthew 24 passage that His followers will go through a period of intense persecution up until the Abomination of Desolation.

Some have tried to argue that the first portion of Matthew 24 speaks of events that led up to the destruction of the Second Temple and the Roman exile. This view is in conflict with the context which Matthew 24:3 provides, for in this verse the disciples inquired of Yeshua concerning when the end of the age would be. What Rome did which led to the destruction of the Temple does not fit the description of other portions of the first section of Matthew chapter 24, for this conflict was a Jewish revolt against the Roman Empire and not a war involving numerous nations, like verses six and seven state.

In returning to the imminency issue, there is another point that one must consider when asserting that the Rapture takes place after the Abomination of Desolation. For those who adhere to the imminency doctrine, such a statement seems to violate its very core. This is because if the Abomination of Desolation must take place prior to the Rapture, this would mean that until this event happens, the Rapture would not be imminent. However, if one remembers that the Scriptural basis for the imminency doctrine does not state that the Rapture is actually imminent, but only that one will not know the day or hour of the Rapture, then the view that the Abomination of Desolation must precede the Rapture does not actually violate the Scriptural mandate for which the doctrine is based. This reality should satisfy those who embrace the doctrine of imminency, but they then in turn argue that imminency would not become a reality until after the Abomination of Desolation takes place and not prior—hence making Yeshua's statement not accurate until after the Abomination of Desolation happens. Once again, their problem is equating not knowing the day or hour with imminency, rather that understanding Yeshua's words for what they actually say.

The Rapture as Deliverance

Most students of the Bible understand that an additional outcome of the Rapture is that it removes believers from the earth immediately prior to the wrath of G-d falling. In the previous chapter, it was demonstrated that it is the wrath of G-d which becomes imminent during the sixth seal of Revelation chapter six. It was also stated that during the sixth seal the sun would become black and the moon like blood prior to G-d's wrath falling. It was also shown how this parallels Joel's prophecy, which also included the same description prior to the Day of the L-rd. The reader should conclude that the Day of the L-rd is a period that will begin only after the Abomination of Desolation. The Day of the L-rd should be understood as a time period in which G-d's judgment and wrath is poured out upon the world. It is only from this tribulation, which has as its source the Holy G-d, from which the believer should expect to be delivered.

Whereas believers are delivered from this tribulation, Israel is sealed by G-d and must be sustained during this period. It has already been pointed out that although the sixth seal announces the wrath of the Lamb (Messiah Yeshua), it does not actually fall in chapter six of the book of Revelation. It is only after Israel is sealed in chapter seven, and another most interesting sight in heaven occurs, that G-d's judgment begins to fall. What is this interesting sight and how is it related to the Rapture?

John is provided a vision inside of heaven and what did he see?

> *"After these things I looked and behold a large crowd, which no man was able to count, from every ethnicity, and tribe and people and language were standing before the Throne and before the Lamb, having been clothed in white robes and a palm branch in their hands. And they were crying out with a loud voice saying, 'The salvation of our G-d Who sits upon the Throne and to the Lamb.*" Revelation 7:9-10

I would suggest to the reader, as Marvin Rosenthal did in his book entitled, "Pre-wrath Rapture of the Church", that this vision is of those in heaven who were "raptured" (taken) out of the world prior to the Day of the L-rd. These two verses provide great insight to the reader concerning the faithfulness of the Living G-d to those who trusted in His Messiah. Prior to discussing these verses, it needs to be pointed out that the sealing of Israel to go through the "Great Tribulation" and the Rapture of believers before the Day of the L-rd, speak loudly to the Biblical truth that Israel and the Church are never to be understood as the same entity, nor does the Church replace Israel.

The passage from Revelation chapter seven speaks of a large crowd which consisted of those from a diversity of backgrounds. The terminology employed here leads the reader to conclude that it is a reference to those who have been purchased by the blood of Messiah throughout the ages. This is confirmed by the fact that this crowd is seen standing before the throne of G-d and the Lamb, obviously a reference to Yeshua. The white robes serve to confirm their purity/holiness and the palm branches have great significance based upon Jewish insight. Palm branches were part of the four types of vegetation that the people of G-d were commanded to take in observance of the festival of Tabernacles (See Leviticus 23:39-41). The palm branch was the foundational part for the other three species. That which was made is known in Judaism as a "lulav". This practice is still observed today. When the worshipper takes the lulav he waves it in six different directions. It is understood as a call to the nations to accept the grace of G-d for salvation. Many Christians are aware of the term "Hosannah" and its connection to Messiah's entrance into Jerusalem on what has become known as "Palm Sunday". It is very significant that one takes the lulav while reading from a special group of six Psalms, 113-118. Although the lulav is actually only waved during certain verses, it is worth noting that immediately before the first waving, Psalm 117 is sung. This Psalm is a call for all Gentiles to respond faithfully to this grace of G-d

"Praise the L-rd all Gentiles, laud Him all peoples, for mightily upon us is His grace and the truth of the L-rd is forever; Praise the L-rd." Psalm 117

As the lulav is shaken one sings,

"Give thanks to the L-rd, for He is good; because His mercy endures forever. Let Israel now say, because His mercy endures forever. Let the house of Aaron say, because His mercy endures forever. Let those who fear the L-rd say, because His mercy endures forever." Psalm 118:1-4

Although all of Psalm 118 is recited, the last portion captures the message which Israel is called to proclaim to the world.

"Open for me the gates of righteousness, I will enter through them, I will give thanks to Yah (the L-rd). This is the gate of the L-rd; righteous ones will enter through it. I will give thanks because He has answered me and You have become for me Salvation! The Stone the builders have rejected has become the chief cornerstone; this is from the L-rd, it is wonderful in our eyes. This is the day the L-rd has made, we will rejoice and be glad in Him." Psalm 118:19-24

When arriving at verse 25, the lulav is once again shaken in all directions while singing,

"Please Oh L-rd save us now, Please Oh L-rd make us successful now." Psalm 118:25

This verse is actually what Yeshua's followers said when they shouted, "Hosannah in the highest". It is the summation of the meaning of these verses and the tradition of the lulav which provides an interesting perspective for John's vision in Revelation chapter 7. Those in heaven had responded to the grace which is emphasized when waving the lulav. Judaism understands that the focus of this section is Messiah. It is informative that Psalm 118 states that it is the L-rd Who has become salvation for us (verse 21). This should be understood as a reference to the incarnation. It is also significant that this Psalm mentions the Stone (verse 22). This is the same Stone which Daniel reveals is hurled at the image and destroys it (see Daniel 2:34). One should remember that this Stone is the Messiah. Hence, it is Yeshua Whom Israel's leaders (the builders mentioned in verse 22 of this Psalm) rejected that becomes the chief cornerstone. As the Psalm states, "*This is from the L-rd, it is wonderful in our eyes.*"

The believers who are seen standing in heaven are said not only to be clothed in a white robe, but have a palm branch, i.e. lulav, in their hands. This description emphasizes that it was because they responded properly to the enduring grace of Yeshua, and that they had received Him Who became Salvation, that they were taken away from the earth prior to G-d's wrath falling. It is also significant that the lulav is part of the festival of Tabernacles celebration. This festival reminds one of his absolute dependence on and trust in the L-rd for all things. It was this truth which G-d was teaching to the Israelites during the forty years in the wilderness that was necessary for them to enter into the Promise Land. It is this same truth that each person must learn in order to enter into the Kingdom of G-d.

What Actually Happens When the Rapture Takes Place?

Shortly after the Abomination of Desolation, but before the wrath of G-d begins to fall, those who have accepted the Gospel message of Messiah Yeshua, both dead and alive, will experience a wonderful change. First, the remains of dead believers, no matter where they may be located or in what condition they may be, will miraculously be changed. These remains will rise into the sky along with the bodies of those believers who are alive. These remains, along with those individuals still alive, will be transformed supernaturally and meet Yeshua in the sky where He will take them to heaven. It is important to note that the souls of those who already died have been with Messiah since their death. The fact that the souls of believers immediately rise into heaven at the time of death is supported by several verses. One of them is based in Paul's letter to the Corinthians,

"But we are confident, and we take delight all the more; to be absent from the body and to be at home with the L-rd."
II Corinthians 5:8

The nature of this transformation is clearly revealed in First Corinthians chapter 15. There Paul comments about the bodies of birds, fish, animals, and man. He points out that each of these bodies were specifically designed by G-d for their individual habitation. This truth lays the foundation for what he wants to teach concerning the new body which believers will receive at the Rapture. We shall inherit a body designed by G-d for eternal life in the Kingdom; in other words, a body which is immortal and one that will not experience any corruption or decay. This new body will not be able to sin and will always know the will of G-d. This fact is derived from what the L-rd intended to do with the Children of Israel after revealing the Ten Commandments at Mount Sinai.

"And Moses said to the people, 'Do not fear, for in order to bring upon a new experience, G-d is coming, in order that His fear will be before you and you will not be able to sin."
Exodus 20:20

It is very important that one notices that when the L-rd offered the Children of Israel this opportunity to be transformed, it was accompanied by the sound of the shofar (Ram's horn) according to Exodus 20:18. The shofar was first referenced in the book of

Genesis, in the section where the L-rd commands Abraham to sacrifice his son Isaac (Genesis 22). After being told by the angel not to kill Isaac, Abraham was provided a ram, which was caught in the thicket by his horns. The shofar is a special type of "trumpet", which although is used for many different purposes, there are two primary meanings attached to the sounding of the shofar. The first is to remember what G-d has provided. For Abraham and Isaac, the ram which was provided represented life. For if the L-rd had not provided the ram as a substitute for Isaac, the result would have been Isaac's death and the removing of the hope which was rooted in this child of promise. The second significance learned from the shofar is contained in the word "shofar". As has been noted previously, Hebrew words have their origin from "root words" which provide a foundation for understanding the word which is derived from its root. In this case, the word "shofar" originates from a word which means "to improve". Hence, the sounding of the shofar is often understood in Judaism to be a call to repentance. Obviously, true repentance represents a spiritual improvement. The key point one must remember is that a person can only improve by means of what G-d has provided man. Judaism understands this to ultimately be the redemption which will be brought by the Messiah.

It is not a coincidence that at the time of the Rapture not only will Messiah descend from heaven, but the reader is also informed that when He does so He will be accompanied by the sounding of the shofar (See I Thessalonians 4:16-17). This occurrence is to teach the reader that one will be part of the Rapture and the benefits thereof, only if he receives G-d's provision of redemption achieved by Messiah's death. The new body one will receive represents not only an improvement, but the perfection of man, so that believers can rule and reign with Messiah in the Kingdom (See Revelation 20:4).

Chapter 8

"Great Tribulation"

It is necessary to remember that a distinction must be made between the types of tribulation that will occur in the end times. It has already been stated that this distinction lies in the source of the tribulation, whether it is satanic or divine. Although there is today, and has been satanic tribulation since the Garden of Eden, in the end times this type of tribulation will greatly increase, leading up to the final seven year period and especially in the first half this period. However, soon after the Abomination of Desolation a great tribulation will begin. When examining the Scriptures, there are two passages which contain a reference to great tribulation. Yet when investigating these passages, one finds that they are not referring to the same period of time.

The first passage is found in Matthew chapter 24. It is significant that this section of Scripture is addressed to those who are in Judea and takes place immediately after the reference to the Abomination of Desolation in verse 15.

"For there will be then great tribulation, which has not been from the beginning of the world until now nor shall ever take place." Matthew 24:21

This verse informs the reader that the worst period ever for the Jewish people will be at the end of this age. This means worse than the Holocaust. Daniel chapter 12 speaks to this same matter,

"And at that time will stand Michael, the great prince (of the angels), *who stands for Your people; and there will be a time of tribulation which has not been since a nation* (existed) *unto that time, and in that time Your people will escape, all who are found written in the book."* Daniel 12:1

The reference in this verse to "a nation" relates to Israel; therefore Daniel also is confirming that this will indeed be Israel's most trying period of persecution. Yet, similar to Jeremiah's statement about this same period which he calls a time for Jacob's Trouble (See Jeremiah 30:7), in the end Israel (a remnant) will find salvation.

The second passage is found in Revelation chapter seven. This passage has already been discussed when examining the Rapture. When John sees those who have been "raptured" out of this world and are now standing in heaven before G-d's throne and before the Lamb (Messiah), he does not know who they are. He is informed that "*These are the ones who have come out of the great tribulation, and have washed their robes* (and) *made them white by means of the blood of the Lamb*." (See Revelation 7:13-17).

Whereas it is clear that those from the Matthew 24 passage relate to Israel, these found in the book of Revelation are believers. The reference to them having utilized the blood of the Lamb confirms this. The question which must be asked is, "how can one be sure that the Matthew passage speaks about an event after the Abomination of Desolation, while the Revelation passage speaks of an event prior to the Abomination of Desolation, when the same term 'great tribulation' is used in both passages?" The answer is that the same term is not in fact used in both passages. Although the same Greek words are used in both places, the Matthew passage does not utilize the definite article, while the one in Revelation does. In other words, in Matthew, Yeshua is saying that those in Judea (Israel) will have great tribulation, while in Revelation, the use of the definite article means that the period should be known by the title, "The Great Tribulation".

In this chapter the focus will be on the period of tribulation which will take place after the Abomination of Desolation, whose source is divine in origin. Although Israel and the Jewish people in general will suffer greatly, so too will the entire world. One must remember all the while, that believers have finished their time of persecution and are in heaven. Another important fact is that the Gospel was proclaimed during the last two thousand years primarily to the Gentiles; however, during the second half of Daniel's 70th week, (the final seven years prior to Messiah's return and establishing His Kingdom), G-d will move in a variety of ways to bring Jewish individuals to faith in the same Gospel.

The Seven Trumpets

Thus far, the first six seals of the book of Revelation have been examined. In this chapter, the seventh seal, which contains seven specific events which relate to divine judgment, will be studied. These seven different occurrences of G-d's wrath are known as the "Seven Trumpets". Perhaps a better way of identifying these seven trumpets is with the term "Seven Shofarot". Since the term shofar relates to both G-d's provision for life and a call to repentance, this term may speak more to the purpose of these judgments. Prior to the first shofar/trumpet being sounded, one reads,

"*...and there came about sounds, and thunder and lightning and earthquakes.*" Revelation 8:5

Such things as these are often used to convey a message to the reader. Eschatological literature uses these terms to announce a change or a new reality. A good student of the book of Revelation will notice that the word "throne" appears numerous (thirty-six) times. The sounds, thunder, lightning and earthquakes foreshadow the transition that is taking place as G-d begins to bring about the changes in this world so that He can place His throne in Jerusalem. G-d dwelling personally among man is the primary purpose of redemption,

"*I will place My tabernacle in your midst and My soul will not reject you. I will walk in your midst and I will be for you G-d and you shall be for Me a people. I am the L-rd your G-d Who brought you from the land of Egypt...*" Leviticus 26:11-13

In this passage G-d's desire to have a personal and intimate relationship with man is clearly seen. It is significant that after stating this, there is a reference to the Exodus from Egypt, a type of redemption. Earthquakes are also mentioned in the Revelation passage as a way of communicating to the reader that G-d's judgment, and the purpose for these judgments, concerns the entire world. When examining the trumpet judgments, the number one-third appears over and over. The reader should conclude from this that G-d's wrath, which is being poured out on the earth, is not for the purpose of utterly destroying the earth and its residents, but as one will see at the conclusion of these judgments, a call for all to repent and embrace the redemption that G-d has offered the world, by means of the Gospel.

When the first shofar sounds, hail and fire, mixed with blood fell from heaven. Many of the events in the book of Revelation are often times explained by scholars as things which are not supernatural, but are simply the result of things which were not known or even existed at the time of John. This book will take a strongly different perspective. It is the opinion of this writer that it is in fact G-d, and G-d alone, Who is causing these events and not just using the deeds of man to accomplish His purposes. One should understand that the primary motivation of these judgments is not only to punish the wickedness of man, but to also capture the attention of those who survive these judgments in the hope that they would turn to the Gospel and repent. The result of the first shofar is that one-third of the trees were burned up and all the grass was consumed.

The fact that the Scripture does not mention any physical suffering of man as a direct result of the hail and fire mixed with blood falling is quite amazing. Certainly the outcome of such destruction would in fact bring suffering to humans, but the point that no man actually was harmed by the initial falling, shows a miraculous aspect to this judgment. In other words, people should see G-d's hand in this judgment and perceive His mercy.

Next, the second shofar sounds and an even more spectacular phenomenon takes place. A great mountain, burning with fire, was cast into the sea. The intent here is probably the Mediterranean Sea with the result that all seas and oceans were affected in the same way—one-third of the water became blood. Due to this, one-third of sea life died as well as one-third of the ships was destroyed. Once again, this is not something which could be explained by natural factors. This judgment is clearly a divine occurrence. It is obvious that these two judgments would cause a major catastrophe for the world. Also, the likelihood that these trumpets are sounding one after another, would only serve to intensify the devastation. Without any hesitation, the third shofar sounds, and that which resembles a star falls from the heavens. The reader is told it appears as a burning lamp. This star-like object strikes one-third of the rivers and natural reservoirs of water. This description defies logic, yet this is exactly what is going to take place. Although humanity will have already been greatly suffering due to the first two judgments, and it is highly reasonable to conclude that countless deaths have occurred, it is only as a result of this third judgment that the text states explicitly that people die. The star is given the name "Wormwood", which relates to the fact that it turns one-third of the water bitter and many people died from drinking this water.

This is not the first time that people encountered bitter water. Israel, during her forty year journey in the wilderness, experienced bitter waters (See Exodus 15:22-27). Obviously the people would want a solution to the water problem. With more and more people dying, the situation would be quite dire. It is most important to remember how Moses solved the problem during the Exodus. The text states that Moses was shown a tree which he cast into the bitter waters and supernaturally they became drinkable. What is the message of this story and how does it relate to that which will happen in the future? Water often times represents life; the bitterness that characterized the waters, would relate to the horrible period of time humanity was experiencing due to these divine judgments. The tree which was cast into the bitter waters is a reference to the Cross of Messiah, for it is only His work of redemption upon the Cross which can transform a life, made bitter by sin, into a life which is truly satisfying.

The fourth shofar is most different than the previous three. Instead of some actual physical judgment which brings about a major crisis upon the world, this judgment is only a proclamation. Remembering that a primary objective of these judgments is to cause humanity to give consideration to G-d and repent, it is not surprising that the event of the fourth shofar is absolutely unable to be explained through any natural occurrence.

"And the fourth angel sounded, and was struck a third of the sun and a third of the moon and a third of the stars, in order that a third of them should become dark, and in the day a third of the light would not shine, and likewise in the night. And I looked and I heard one of the angels flying in the midst of the heavens saying in a great voice, 'Woe, Woe, Woe, to those who dwell upon the earth, because of the remaining soundings of the shofarot, by the three angels which are about to sound.'" Revelations 8:12-13

Imagine the horror of all the residents of the earth after experiencing the first three judgments, hearing that these calamities were only preparation for three worse ones yet to come.

The First Woe

When the fifth angel sounded his shofar, one like a star descended from the heavens to earth. This one was given a special key that unlocked the Abyss. This Abyss is likened to a great pit from which both smoke and a unique type of locusts ascended. These locusts were given special power like scorpions, but did not do damage to any type of vegetation or trees. Rather, these locusts with their scorpion-like tails stung only humans. This plague lasted for five months and although it did not cause death, it was so painful that people desired to die; yet death was said to flee from the people, meaning that there was no way for one to escape this judgment. There was, however, one group of people these locusts did not sting. These were those who had the seal of G-d; in other words, those of Jewish decent. This provision is most similar to how G-d shielded the Hebrews in Egypt during the plagues.

The description of the locusts makes it very clear that these are not some ordinary type of locusts; they were shaped like a horse and had many other peculiar features (See Revelation 9:1-11). Due to the fact that they rose from the Abyss, and had a ruler over them called "the Destroyer", it is most reasonable to conclude that these locusts are a type of demon. Because those who were not taken in the Rapture were ones who did not respond in faith to the plan of G-d (the Gospel), now the L-rd is turning them over to Satan so that he can do what he delights to do to all people, i.e., torture. Jewish individuals, although no more obedient to G-d's plans and purposes, are spared as a way of showing both them and the Gentiles that G-d does indeed make a distinction between Israel and the rest of the nations. This distinction should not be viewed as favoritism, but as a call. In the same way that there was a mixed multitude in Egypt who bonded with Israel and kept the Passover and left Egypt with Israel, this distinction which G-d is making with the Jewish people is for the purpose of calling the Gentiles to unite with them. When a Gentile does so, he becomes a recipient of the same blessings and treatment that any Jewish individual receives.

If one errs and believes that Christians replace Israel, and there is no longer any special call for the sons of Jacob, then as it shall be demonstrated, the book of Revelation, as well as many other Scriptures, become impossible to understand unless one allegorizes and applies methods of Biblical interpretation which open the way for others to spiritualize away the uniqueness and authority of Messiah Yeshua. It is interesting that many who use as a pretext the superiority of Christ as a way of rejecting the literal interpretation of the Prophets, actually undermine His Superiority by discounting the simple meaning of the text. In other words, the methodology which the Replacement theologians apply to the Prophets, when also applied to the New Testament, provides those who want to discount the words of the Gospel writers and the Apostles with the tools and ammunition to undermine their message.

With the conclusion of the five months of torment from the "locusts", the reader is told that the first Woe is over and two more shall follow.

The Second Woe

The sixth angel sounded his shofar and a voice was heard coming from the four horns of the golden altar. Because it is stated that this altar is before G-d, it is proper to conclude that this altar is from the heavenly Temple. With the sounding of the shofar, the reader is told that four angels are loosed who have been bound in the Euphrates River. These angels will bring about an attack upon humanity by 200 million soldiers. Once again, in the same way that the locusts were not ordinary locusts, these soldiers were not ordinary soldiers. They also resembled horses, but had heads like lions and from their mouths came forth fire, smoke, and brimstone. By means of these three (fire, smoke, and brimstone) they killed a third of mankind.

A most interesting piece of information is provided to the reader when he is told that despite all the suffering and horrible things that the survivors witnessed up until this time, when given the opportunity to repent they would not do so. Not only are these individuals involved in idolatry, murder, sorcery, sexual immorality, and theft, but also in the worship of demons. It was immediately after failing to repent that another angel is seen descending from the heaven. This angel had a little book and when he arrived to earth he placed his right foot in the sea and his left on land. Instead of revealing the things written in this little book, the angel is commanded to seal up the book. The text actually states the angel was told not to write anything in the book that he heard from the "seven thunders". What these "seven thunders" are is difficult to say. However, the point here is that there is no revelation concerning the specific events which will take place at this time.

What is revealed is that these events which the "seven thunders" uttered contained the various events that will bring about a significant outcome—that the MYSTERY OF G-D should be complete. What is this mystery? The only thing that is certain concerning this mystery is that it relates to what G-d revealed to the Prophets. John requests to be given the book. Many scholars state that this request implies a desire by him to know this mystery. The angel who was holding the little book did in fact give it to John, but not so he could discern anything, rather he is commanded to eat the book. This book, although sweet in his mouth, was sour in his stomach. Although it is only speculation, it may mean that the final results of the prophecy would be sweet, i.e. joyful, but the means of this prophecy being fulfilled were difficult and sad.

The term "mystery" occurs numerous times in the Scriptures, however the term "MYSTERY OF G-D" is only found in one other verse. In Paul's Epistle to the Colossians, he writes a sentence that has numerous variants. That is, there are several families of manuscripts which have different renderings for the phrase in question. However when one considers all the evidence that is available to scholars today, the best translation for this verse from Colossians 2:2 is,

"In order that their hearts should be comforted and united together in love, and in all fullness of assurance of the understanding in the acknowledgment of the mystery of G-d which is Messiah."

So it is Messiah Who is the Mystery of G-d. At first thought this seems somewhat odd, because the concept of Messiah was well known in Judaism, so why would Paul in the Colossians passage, and John in Revelation, be referring to Messiah as the Mystery of

G-d? The answer is that they were not simply referring to the Messiah in a general sense, but to the fact that Messiah would suffer in order to redeem Israel. When John writes about this mystery he says, "...*which the Prophets declared*"; yet most did not take the verses from the Prophets which foretold of a suffering Servant to heart. Israel expected a delivering king and gave very little attention to how the Messiah was going to accomplish atoning for sin. It was to this fact that Paul spoke when he said,

"...*until this day I have stood bearing witness to small and great, no other thing saying but that also which the Prophets and Moses spoke should happen; destined to suffer is the Messiah.*" Acts 26:22-23a

Although many have tried to share this truth with the Jewish people, very little in roads have been made. It is estimated less than one percent of Israelis believe in Yeshua as the Messiah. What will bring about dramatic change in this condition?

The Two Witnesses

Although John, in a personal way, will not be given the specifics about how Israel will come to recognize the Messiah, John does address the period of time when this will take place. In fact, he has been speaking about the second half of Daniel's 70th week (the last seven years prior to the establishment of the millennial Kingdom) for several chapters. In Revelation chapter 11, there is a clear focus upon the city of Jerusalem. When one examines this chapter, it speaks concerning the entire final half of the seven year period of great tribulation. John is given a reed to measure the Temple and the altar and those who worship there. He is told emphatically **not** to measure the outer court. This is because the court and the city will be in the possession of the Gentiles and they will trample it for 42 months (the final three and a half years). This is indeed the period known in Jeremiah 30:7 as "Jacob's Trouble". It is in the midst of this persecution from the

Gentiles that the Jewish people will be confronted with testimony from two witnesses.

"And I will give to My two witnesses and they shall prophesy one thousand two hundred and sixty days, having been clothed in sackcloth." Revelation 11:3

It is not specifically revealed what they are given or who it is that is giving it to them. However, because the Gentiles want to kill them, but are unable to do so until they finish their prophesying, most understand that it is G-d Who provided them the words and the power to declare unto Israel a special message until they have completed this task. The reader is informed that anyone who attempts to harm these witnesses will be killed by fire which shoots forth from their mouths. Although one cannot be dogmatic about whom these two witnesses are, there does tend to be some internal evidence from chapter 11 that they are Moses and Elijah. This is because the reader is told that they can shut the heavens so that it will not rain and they can turn the waters into blood. The first of these acts Elijah was known to have done, while the latter Moses did in Egypt. Elijah is prophesied to return prior to the Coming of Messiah (See Malachi 3:22-24) and Moses is also mentioned in this same passage.

It is clear from verse eight of chapter 11 that the two witnesses share their testimony in Jerusalem, but the spiritual condition of this city has declined so as to be likened to Sodom and Egypt. Once the two witnesses finish their testimony, they are immediately killed by the beast. It is most significant that the text states that the beast will make war with them and overcome them and kill them, as this is what the beast had done with believers in the first half of the seven year period. The similarity in language should cause the reader to unite the two witnesses with the believers. This makes a very strong case that the prophecy which the two witnesses were sharing was the Gospel. The fact that they laid dead in the streets for a full three days and then rose from the dead is like Yeshua, Who was in the tomb three full days. This similarity should confirm to the reader that indeed the two witnesses were proclaiming the Gospel to Israel.

Messiah, when speaking about His purpose for coming into the world stated,

> "*Do not think that I came to cast peace upon the earth; I came not to cast peace, but a sword.*" Matthew 10:34

Why would Yeshua say such a thing? If one studies the context that follows in this section of Matthew chapter ten, it is division. Yeshua speaks about the enmity that will be between people, even within a family. It is not surprising that in the parallel passage from Luke's Gospel, the word "sword" is replaced with the word "division". Prior to this statement about bringing a sword or division, Yeshua spoke about a baptism. His reference to baptism is not in regard to that which took place in the Jordan River, but Yeshua is relating the concept of baptism to His death, burial, and resurrection. It is Yeshua's death, burial, and resurrection that are the basis for the Gospel.

Not only did the two witnesses rise from the dead, they even gave a picture of the Rapture when the text states,

> "*And they heard a great voice out of the heaven saying to them, 'Come up here!' And they ascended into the heaven in a cloud and their enemies perceived them.*" Revelation 11:12

As one examines this chapter, it becomes very clear that these two witnesses were called to testify concerning the identity of the Messiah and His work of redemption and concerning those who followed Him. Both Yeshua and His followers suffered in faithfulness to G-d, as now these two witnesses did also. It should now be obvious to those who rejoiced and sent gifts to one another in celebration of the two witnesses' death, that such behavior was in opposition to the will of G-d, as was the persecution of believers. This should have been readily seen when G-d called these two witnesses up to heaven to be with Him. After the ascension of the two witnesses, an earthquake happened and a tenth part of the city was destroyed, killing seven thousand men. It is at this time that there is a change in the people, as it is said that a remnant feared and gave glory to G-d. With this statement the reader is told that the second Woe has passed, but the third and final one is coming quickly.

Chapter 11 concludes with the seventh angel sounding the seventh shofar. A voice was heard from heaven with a glorious proclamation,

> *"The kingdoms of the world have become of our L-rd's and of His Messiah and He will reign forever and ever."*
>
> Revelation 11:15

It is very significant that in the next verse, 24 elders are mentioned. Obviously this number, as will be seen when studying the New Jerusalem, is based upon the 12 tribes of Israel and the 12 apostles. These elders not only worship G-d at this time, but also point out that He is beginning His administration upon earth. They emphasize that His wrath has come and that He will judge those who stood in opposition to His will and that He will reward His Prophets and the saints who feared His name. The final image of chapter 11 is that of the heavenly Temple. Just like in every synagogue in the world, the primary object is the ark, which contains the Torah. It is this Ark of the Covenant that is singled out. When the term covenant is mentioned it is a reference to the Torah. Why is John receiving this vision? The Torah represents the standards of G-d. While one is redeemed solely on the basis of faith in the Gospel, by means of Grace, judgment is by means of the standards which are revealed in the Word of G-d.

When speaking of the Torah, Moses was instructed to reveal to the Children of Israel that, depending on one's response to the Word of G-d, he would either be blessed or cursed (See Deuteronomy 30:11-20). This is what is going to take place now as G-d begins to rule in this world. It is important to note that this transition from the prince of this age, i.e. Satan, to the righteous rule of Messiah Yeshua is not immediate, but there are several things which must transpire. It is the final Woe which contains these events which will end with the return of Messiah to earth. Once again there is a mention of lightning, voices (perhaps the sound of the shofar sounding), thunder, hail, and an earthquake. As has previously been discussed, such things announce a change that is about to take place.

With the conclusion of chapter 11 the book of Revelation ends the chronological progression that began in chapter four. When one examines chapter 12 he encounters a new section that is found in chapters 12, 13 and 14. This section basically recounts the events of chapters four through eleven. What is the purpose of this recounting and what can one learn from it? This is the subject of the next section.

Chapter 9

"Revelation Chapters 12-14"

There cannot be any disagreement that Revelation chapter 12 looks back to a very unique presentation of Messiah's birth and a conflict which began in the heavens and spread to the earth. The victory of believers is also clearly revealed, as well as the means of this victory. The dichotomy between the Church and Israel is also plainly shown. In short, this 12th chapter restates in great brevity what John saw in numerous visions. It is vital for one to review this chapter in order to confirm his understanding of the previous visions before moving on to new material.

The chapter opens up with what is called a great wonder of heaven. The first thing which is said concerning this wonder is that there is a woman. This woman will be in contrast to the whore that is related to the beast. When examining this woman, it becomes evident that she depicts Israel. The reference to the sun and the moon and 12 stars are borrowed from Joseph's dream in Genesis chapter 37. The woman is said to be ready to give birth and the Child who would be born was said,

> "...to rule all nations with a rod of iron and her Child was taken to G-d and to His throne." Revelation 12:5

It is beyond all doubt that the woman represents Israel and, of course, the Child is the Messiah. In opposition to the woman (Israel) and the Child Who was to be born, is a great red dragon. The reader is told that the dragon has seven heads and ten horns. Had the reader failed to make the connection between the beast and Satan previously, it is now impossible to fail to understand that the beast in the end times, as well as those who persecuted Israel throughout the ages, are absolutely related to Satan. The war that was in heaven between Satan and Michael and his angels resulted in Satan and a third of the angels he lured to himself to be cast out of heaven. Furthermore, the reader is told that the dragon was waiting for the woman to give birth so that he could devour the Child (See verse 4).

One should not fail to notice that the same hate which is aimed at the Messiah is also directed toward the woman (Israel). It is due to this persecution against Israel that it is said that she will flee into the wilderness, to a place prepared by G-d, where He will provide for her for a period of 1,260 days. This duration of time is also referred to as 42 months (See verse six). It is clear that this period of time is after the Abomination of Desolation. The time period which this vision is referring to is "Jacob's Trouble". This information parallels what is said by Yeshua Himself in Matthew chapter 24. Immediately after the Abomination of Desolation, there would be those in Judea who would flee into the wilderness (See Matthew 24:16-21).

In returning to the fact that Satan and his angels have been cast to the earth, there is a powerful statement that the only way by which one can experience victory over Satan's persecution and plan is found in verse 11.

"And they overcame him by means of the blood of the Lamb and by means of the word of their testimony, and they did not love their life to death."

In the latter section of this chapter there is a restating that Israel will be sustained in the wilderness from the attacks of Satan for a period of time. Concerning this time, instead of mentioning either 1,260 days or 42 months, a phrase from the book of Daniel is borrowed, "a time, and times, and a half of time" (See Daniel 7:25). This expression is equivalent to three and a half years. After concluding this section about how Satan will war with Israel, there is a return to a discussion of the beast. The bridge between the section discussing the dragon's hatred and persecution against Israel and the overview of the activity of the beast is found in the last verse of chapter 12.

"And the dragon was angry with the woman and went out to make war with the remaining ones of her seed; the ones that keep the commandments of G-d and have the testimony of Messiah Yeshua." Revelation 12:17

One needs to pay close attention to the fact that chapter 12 provided the reader with an overview of the purpose for identifying the major entities in the book of Revelation. These entities are Israel, the Messiah, believers, the beast, the nations (inhabitants of the earth), and Satan. After making it clear to the reader exactly to whom these visions relate, the objective of John is to provide a summary of what has taken place in the earlier chapters and to offer some specific insight concerning these events. Next, chapter 13 will be addressed.

This study has already utilized this chapter in many instances to assist in understanding the nature and character of the beast. It was also useful in supporting the fact that believers will be intensely persecuted by the beast and that the beast will establish a rule over the entire world (See verses five through seven). Another important characteristic that was learned is that the beast is not secular in nature, but desires to be worshipped by all (See verse eight). Chapter 13 pays special attention to believers, called saints, rather than upon Israel. In the second half of chapter 13 another beast is mentioned. This beast was already identified as the Antichrist. It is under his leadership of the beast (empire) that believers in Yeshua will suffer this intense persecution. It was shown earlier in our study that this period of tribulation is during the first half of the seven year period. This fact is important in not erring when one arrives at the vision of the following chapter.

Revelation Chapter 14

This chapter begins with a vision of the Lamb, i.e., Messiah, standing on Mount Zion and with Him was a group of 144,000 individuals. Who are these people? There are reasons at first glance to associate them with the 144,000 in Revelation chapter seven. Those were clearly Jewish individuals who were sealed prior to the wrath of G-d being poured out. The sealing was to preserve them during the time of Jacob's Trouble. The fact that the number (144,000) is the same and like in chapter seven, both groups had a seal upon their foreheads, it would be natural to assume that both chapters are speaking about the same group. However, closer examination of the text proves otherwise.

Normally one should take the Scripture in a literal manner unless there is strong indication to view it as symbolic. When speaking about the 144,000 from chapter seven it was pointed out that the number 12 represents the people of G-d. Hence, the number 144 is 12 x 12. In the text from chapter seven, the L-rd sealed 12,000 from each of the 12 tribes. The number 1,000 is a multiple of the number ten which relates to "wholeness", "totality", or completeness". Therefore, it was suggested that the number 144,000 related not to a literal 144,000 Jews, but a symbolic number representing all of Israel alive at that period of time.

In a similar manner in chapter 14, the 144,000 also represents the people of G-d in some complete manner. One should pay attention to what is said concerning this 144,000 in chapter 14. First, they are said to be with Messiah on Mount Zion. How is Mount Zion understood in the Scripture? One early occurrence of the term Zion is,

"*For from Jerusalem will go forth a remnant and refugees from Mount Zion; the zeal of the L-rd shall do this.*"
II Kings 19:31

In several other places, this same idea of escape or deliverance is found located with the term "Mount Zion".

"*And it shall be that all who call on the Name of the L-rd will escape; for in Mount Zion and in Jerusalem there shall be refugees, just as the L-rd said, 'And with the survivors whom the L-rd calls.*" Joel 3:5 (Hebrew Bible) Joel 2:32 (English translations)

"For from Jerusalem shall go forth a remnant and refugees from Mount Zion; the zeal of the L-rd of Hosts will do this."

Isaiah 37:32

"And on Mount Zion there shall be refugees and it shall be holy and the house of Jacob shall inherit their heritage."

Obadiah 17

It needs to be pointed out that many well-known translations often times translate the same word in a variety of ways. Because of the great similarity of these verses in message, and due to the fact that the same vocabulary was used, I translated the same Hebrew word with the same English word. The idea of deliverance is certainly appropriate for the Revelation 14:1 passage. Mount Zion is also seen in the Scripture as a place where G-d dwells, so intimacy is also a concept that this verse expresses,

*"And I looked and behold a Lamb standing on Mount Zion and **with Him** one hundred and forty-four thousand, having His Father's name, having been written upon their foreheads."*

The term which I emphasized in this verse, "**with Him**", demonstrates this intimacy. It is also stated that only these 144,000 could learn the song which was heard coming from heaven (See verse three). Most scholars understand this singing as relating to worship; hence only those who share intimacy with the Lamb and have experienced His deliverance are able to worship G-d. These are also said to be virgins, having not been defiled with women. There are many who take this verse literally; however, such an interpretation is somewhat problematic. Does being with a woman defile a man? Man is commanded to be fruitful and multiply and G-d uses marriages to reflect His relationship with Israel and Messiah's relationship with believers. Therefore, there must be more to the term "virgins" in this verse.

Throughout the Bible, those who engage in idolatry are likened to adulterers. Infidelity to G-d is seen as promiscuity; hence the proper intent of likening these 144,000 to virgins is to attest to their faithfulness to G-d and His Word. This is exactly what is expressed in the next verse.

"And in their mouth was not found any deceit; for innocent are they before the Throne of G-d." Revelation 14:5

It is also very important that when one reads in verse six, that there came another angel who had the eternal Gospel to preach to them, the "them" that is mentioned is not the 144,000, but those who dwell upon the earth of every nation, tribe, language, and people. This group is said to dwell upon the earth, while the 144,000 had been redeemed from the earth (See verses three and four). When considering verses seven to eleven, one finds that a proclamation of judgment is the predominant theme. Within this message of judgment is a call to repent and to worship G-d. It is most significant that it is only after the Gospel is offered is this invitation to repent and worship offered. Also in this section is a declaration that Babylon is fallen.

Immediately after the proclamation of the coming judgment and the wrath of G-d, one reads the following verse,

"Here is the patience of the saints; here are those who keep the commandments of G-d and faith of Yeshua."

Revelation 14:12

This is clearly a call to persevere and endure faithfully. It is vital that one understands that the One Who defines this group is Yeshua. The next verse informs them that to die for Him is a blessing and part of their calling. The question which must be asked is how can one be sure that the 144,000 is a reference to the Church and not to a remnant of Israel, or Israel in general, who will come to faith in the midst of their time of affliction (See Jeremiah 30:7)? The answer is found in the next section.

"And I looked and behold a white cloud and upon the cloud was set One like the Son of Man, having upon His head a golden crown and in His hand a sharp sickle. And another angel came out from the sanctuary, crying in a great voice to

*Him Who sat upon the cloud, 'Thrust Your sickle and reap;
because the hour has come for You to harvest because the
harvest of the earth has been made ripe. And the One Who
was set upon the cloud cast His sickle into the earth and the
earth was reaped."* Revelation 14:14-16

This passage describes the Rapture. The depiction of One like the
Son of Man is taken from Daniel 7: 13. There, it was a reference
to the Messiah; and so also in this passage. Messiah has been
placed on a cloud and waits for a message from the Heavenly
Sanctuary, i.e. from G-d His Father via the angel, which the time
has come to harvest the earth. This waiting for the instruction
from G-d the Father may be in fulfillment of Matthew 24:36,
which states only the Father knows the day and the hour. The
point which must be emphasized is that verses 14-16 are not in
reference to judgment. In fact, if one remembers the section
concerning Messiah's resurrection occurring on the first day of
the harvest period, he will be reminded that believers were
depicted as "the harvest"!

Notice that, immediately after the reference to the Rapture,
there is a clear allusion to G-d's wrath. In this closing section of
chapter 14, a different angel comes forth from the heavenly
Sanctuary with a sickle in his hand. An additional angel, who has
the power over fire, came from the altar. This is a significant fact,
as fire is what the L-rd will use to judge the world when He pours
out His wrath. This angel tells the one who holds the sharp sickle
to thrust his sickle. In this passage it is not for the harvest, but for
the grapes of the vine. This corresponds to the Prophet Joel.

Joel 4:9-21 (3:9-21 English)

This section from Joel is addressed to the nations. It is a call to
prepare for war, because G-d is angry with them for their actions
towards Israel, both the land and the people. Because the nations
want to attack Jerusalem, the most likely way to arrive there is
from the north passing through the Jezreel valley. In this passage,

this valley is called the valley of Jehoshaphat, meaning the valley where the L-rd judges. In speaking about the judgment, Joel writes,

> *"Send forth a sickle for vintage is ripened, come go down because the winepress is full, the wineries overflow; their evil is abundant."* Joel 4:13 (Joel 3:13)

There is much similarity between this verse and what one reads in Revelation 14:18-19. Later on in this section, Joel says that this wrath of G-d will come as the sun and moon become dark and the stars do not give their light (see verse 15). This parallels what is said by Yeshua in Matthew chapter 24 concerning His Second Coming. Throughout the book of Revelation, John often was inspired to take motifs and prophecies from the Old Testament and either quote them directly or allude to them clearly in relaying his visions. The closing verses of Revelation chapter 14 are no exception.

Whereas Joel emphasizes how the winepress and the wineries overflow with great amounts of wine, John states this same idea with these words,

> *"And the winepress was trod upon outside the city and the blood went out of the winepress unto the bridle of horses for a thousand and six hundred stadiums."* Revelation 14:20

A stadium is a distance of approximately 200 meters; hence, blood flowed for a distance of 300 kilometers or approximately 200 miles. The fact that not only did the blood reach such a distance is incredible, but also that it was nearly two meters deep. In the final eight verses of the prophecy of Joel, the term Zion appears three times. Each of these occurrences is related to the L-rd's presence in Zion. In other words, prior to G-d establishing His throne in this world, from Jerusalem, i.e. Zion, He must first rid the world from evil. It is for this purpose that His wrath is poured out. This fact is supported by Joel, who says that by means of G-d's wrath that "Jerusalem with be holy". It is within this context that Joel also states that the L-rd will dwell in Zion.

A Message for Today

When Joel writes about G-d's wrath, one should be aware that a major cause of this wrath is how the nations treated Israel in regard to Israel's inheritance. Within the same context of G-d bringing the people to the valley of Jehoshaphat in the latter portion of chapter four (chapter three for English readers), he also prophesies earlier,

> "*And I will gather all the nations and will bring them down to the valley of Jehoshaphat and I will be judged with them there concerning My people and My inheritance Israel which they dispersed among the nations and My land which they divided.*" Joel 4:2 (Joel 3:2)

This verse is clearly speaking about the end times. There are those who want to deny this fact by pointing out that Peter, in his message concerning Pentecost, quoted this section of Joel (See Acts 2:16-21). Peter used this section to explain that which was taking place in Jerusalem that day was a result of the giving of the Holy Spirit. Since Pentecost, one can state that the world has entered into the "last days"; that is, the message of redemption by means of Messiah Yeshua is now available. Joel states,

> "*And it shall be that all who call on the Name of the L-rd will escape; for in Mount Zion and in Jerusalem there shall be refugees, just as the L-rd said, 'And with the survivors whom the L-rd calls.*" Joel 3:5 (Hebrew Bible) Joel 2:32 (English translations)

This is the proclamation which Peter wanted to emphasize to his audience. The time has come where one can, by means of faith in the Gospel, escape the coming wrath which G-d will pour out on this world. The one who does so will not only be saved, but will receive the Holy Spirit. Yet for one to imply that all of Joel's prophecy was fulfilled at Pentecost is hermeneutically invalid.

There is indeed a day coming when G-d's wrath will meet those who dispersed Jews from their land and divided the land (the establishment of a Palestinian State). Is it not informative that Joel states the L-rd is wrathful because of what was done to Israel and not to Palestine? Many translations struggle with the phrase which I translated, "... *and I will be judged with them there concerning My people and My inheritance Israel.*" What does it mean that G-d will be judged with them? The idea here is that one will be able to discern the true nature of G-d when he sees how the L-rd responds to those who mistreated Israel. Joel also states that it is Judah and Jerusalem which will exist forever and not Palestine or Al-Quds. The name Al-Quds is the way Muslims refer to Jerusalem. It is very sad that more and more so-called "Palestinian Christians" (and many Christians in general) are refusing to use the Biblical terms Israel and Jerusalem, and are opting for "Palestine" and "Al-Quds". This growing tendency is reflected in the document entitled "Kairos Palestine". This document was written by "Palestinian Christians" and endorsed by many Christian leaders in general. The following is a quote from this document,

> "...*the establishment of an independent Palestinian state with Al-Quds as its capital.*"

For those who would like to view the document in its entirety, I have supplied the following link:
http://www.kairospalestine.ps/sites/default/Documents/English.pdf

G-d's wrath is indeed coming upon those who reject His Gospel and attempt to thwart His plans.

Chapter 10

"Tribulation Part 2"

With the conclusion of chapter 14, the review of Revelation chapters four through eleven ends; for in chapters 15-18 one learns in great detail the events surrounding and including G-d pouring out His wrath. To those who wish to say that chapter 15 is a continuation of the previous chapter, there is a difficulty which cannot be solved. This difficulty is based in the fact that chapter 14 ends with the wrath of G-d being poured out. So now, in the first verse of the next chapter, how can the very angels who have the seven final plagues of G-d's wrath, still have them to be poured out?

In the next verse there is a clear separation between believers and the rest of the world.

"And I saw a sea of glass having been mixed with fire and those the victorious ones from the beast and from his image and from his mark and from his number of his name stood upon the sea of glass having golden harps." Revelation 15:2

First one needs to remember that the purpose of John's visions is to communicate truth to the reader. It is this final period of tribulation that will see Israel brought to faith and united with others who have placed their faith in the Gospel of the Lamb— Messiah Yeshua. The vision which John receives in the opening verses of chapter 15 conveys this unity between Israel and the Church. The following verse strengthens this point when it is revealed that those who were victorious over the beast sing two songs, the song of Moses, the servant of G-d, and the song of the Lamb (See verse three).

Whereas the judgment of G-d was released by means of the shofarot, the wrath of G-d came by means of "bowls" which were poured out upon the earth, in seven plagues. Another significant distinction between the judgment and the wrath is that the shofarot brought a destruction of only a third; whereas the bowls tended to completely destroy.

The Bowl Judgments

The bowls are said to be full of the wrath of G-d. The word "full" is very telling. This word emphasizes the anger which the L-rd will have for the world. Why is G-d so angry? He is angry because the vast majority of the people will be involved in idolatry. It is also significant to note that most individuals will not survive this period. The first bowl, when it was poured out, caused sores that were uniquely defined in the Greek text. Most translations describe these sores as simply being very painful from a physical standpoint. One cannot over emphasize how grievous these sores will be from such a perspective. However, the Greek text uses two words which normally are used to describe behavior and not physical feelings. This first word describes something bad or evil and the second word usually alludes to something which is morally perverse. Hence, the intent of the verse is not only to emphasize how intense the suffering will be by the recipients of these sores, but also that it was the conduct of these recipients which caused them to receive them. An important principle which can be derived from information provided to the reader by the first bowl judgment is that when one worships improperly, rejecting the instructions of Scripture, this one will live in a manner which will bring upon him the wrath of G-d.

The second bowl is poured out upon the sea. As a result, the water in the sea was turned to blood and all living things in the sea died. The third bowl caused the rivers and reservoirs of water also to turn to blood. With the conclusion of the first three bowls a statement is made concerning the character of G-d. This statement is made by an angel called the angel of waters, who heralds the fact that G-d's righteousness is manifested by His judgment of evil. Also, through this angel's proclamation, one learns why the L-rd turns the waters into blood. It is not a coincidence that the angel who makes this statement is called the angel of waters, nor is it an accident that he speaks concerning the waters. The term "water" conveys two ideas in both rabbinical and Biblical literature. These ideas are "life" and "purity". The term "blood" also relates to life. Therefore it is this angel who praises G-d for avenging the murder of the saints and the prophets—men who spoke the message of life and called people to purity. It was because of this message, which was reflected not just in word, but also in deed, that the beast and those who followed this empire received G-d's wrath.

Even though G-d is love, one should not believe that His love will cause Him to ignore sin and fail to punish sinners. It is precisely because G-d is love and He loves righteousness, holiness, and justice, that He is also wrathful. After the angel of water makes his proclamation, a different angel affirms G-d's actions were based in truth and that righteousness was indeed manifested (See verse seven).

After the proclamations by these two angels, the fourth bowl is poured out. This brought about a change in the sun which caused men to be scorched with fire (heat). Yet, once again, instead of anyone repenting or giving glory to the L-rd, they chose rather to blaspheme the Name of G-d (See verse nine). The fifth angel poured his bowl upon the throne of the beast and his empire became full of darkness. The severe pain which was caused by the fourth bowl continued during this plague of darkness and again there is the emphatic statement that they would not repent from their evil deeds (See verse 11).

It is with the pouring out of the sixth bowl that the most insight is provided to the reader during this period of wrath. Many scholars see an unknown allotment of time passing between the first five bowls and the sixth. The basis for this view is that the rivers, which had been turned to blood, have apparently returned to being water, as one is told that the Euphrates River has water (See verse 12). This bowl is poured out upon the Euphrates and its water is dried up. This occurred in order to provide a way for the kings of the earth to attack Israel.

Armageddon, God, and Magog

Two of the captivating events in the study of prophecy are the battle of Armageddon and the War of Gog and Magog. These two confrontations are in fact one and the same. These terms represent the attack upon Israel that the sixth bowl will prepare. The purpose of this section is not to provide the reader with a detailed interpretation of this event, but to present a general outline of the major points which Scripture reveals concerning this conflict which will end with the Second Coming of the Messiah.

The War of Gog and Magog is prophesied by Ezekiel in chapters 38 and 39 of his prophecy. The first thing one clearly learns is that the L-rd is absolutely opposed to those who approach Israel in order to wage war. Although it is impossible to say with certainty who will be all the major participants in this war, many understand parts of Turkey as being referred to here by the terms Meshech and Tubal. Therefore, in addition to Turkey, one reads that Iran, Ethiopia, and Libya are also part of this coalition to destroy Israel (See verse 5). The reader should understand that the Biblical terms used in this section may in fact include more countries than are actually understood by the names of the modern states. For example, in this section the terms "Persia, Cush, and Put" are mentioned. Even though these designations refer to Iran, Ethiopia, and Libya, the Biblical names include additional lands which the modern states do not possess. For example, the term "Cush" might also include the nations of Sudan and Kenya. Although Ezekiel only names a few countries by name, it is clear that all the world will be standing against Israel and represented in the armies that go up to Israel for war (See verse 9).

It is most interesting how the prophet describes Israel at this time. The Jewish nation is said to be a nation of open towns and of quiet people (See verse 11). In other words, Israel will not be the aggressor in the war nor be the cause. Furthermore, Ezekiel makes it very clear that this battle will take place at the end of this age.

"And you shall go up against My people Israel as a cloud to the land. It shall be in the end times that I will bring you against My land in order that the nations might know Me when I shall be sanctified in you before their eyes O Gog."

Ezekiel 38:16

Gog, being the leader, brings up his coalition of nations to war against Israel. The L-rd will use this battle to demonstrate to the world that the Jewish people are indeed His people and the Land of Israel is His land. In the end, both Gog and his armies will learn the holiness of the G-d of Israel through their defeat. Due to the fact that this prophecy has its fulfillment in the last days, one can make some very interesting conclusions. These conclusions are very problematic for those who hold to a Replacement Theology. Such individuals believe that the right understanding of the term "Israel" is all people who have accepted Messiah Yeshua. Although believers in Yeshua do in fact inherit the promises that G-d made to the natural descendants of Jacob, the prophets did not use such an understanding of the term "Israel" in making their prophecies.

Replacement Theology empties a very important and prevalent message of the Prophets. This message is that G-d will return to the land of Israel and to the natural descendants of Jacob at the end of a period of great tribulation. It is at the end of this period of tribulation that many Jews will be saved (See Jeremiah 30:7). Replacement Theology chooses to ignore such prophecies as Ezekiel Chapters 38 and 39 or interpret them so highly allegorically, that the specifics of the prophecy are unable to be dealt with; rather a general sweeping of the text is made concluding that those in Messiah are the victors.

Applying the views of Replacement Theology to this prophecy means that one should expect in the future that Israel will be populated with a vast majority of believers who will be attacked by the nations at the end of this age. In addition to the unlikeliness that Israel will become a believing nation, prior to the Second Coming, there are other theological problems. Two of these problems are that believers will go through all the tribulation, including the wrath of G-d, and that the Rapture and the Second Coming are same event. Perhaps the greatest obstacle which Replacement theologians must explain is how the deliverance of Israel in the last days against her enemies, which is consummated at the Second Coming, and is the basis for Israel coming to faith, should be understood if "Israel" is, in fact, the Church?

In chapter 39, Ezekiel receives another prophecy about the same war. In this chapter he clearly states that not only will Israel's victory cause Jewish people to recognize the true G-d, but also many of the Gentiles.

> "And My holy Name I will make known in the midst of My people Israel and I will not (allow) any more My holy Name to be profaned. And the Gentiles shall know that I am the L-rd the holy One of Israel." Ezekiel 39:7

A glorious example of G-d's faithfulness is seen in this verse. Since the establishment of the Abrahamic covenant, the L-rd has sworn to use the natural descendants of Jacob in order to bless the Gentiles. Yes, it is Messiah Yeshua and His Gospel, Who is the ultimate fulfiller of this covenant; however it is this war and the deliverance that Israel will receive at Yeshua's Second Coming which will bring the Jewish people by the masses to faith in the Gospel. One should never lose sight that this day of Israel's deliverance will be a powerful message that reveals the character and faithfulness of G-d. The world will witness not only His matchless power, but also His saving grace to Israel and they that survive this battle will likewise repent and embrace Yeshua and

His plan of salvation, for the Jew first and also to the Gentile. This is the proper understanding of Ezekiel's words,

> *"And I will set My glory among the nations and all the Gentiles shall see My judgment which I did and My hand which I placed upon them. And the house of Israel shall know that I am the L-rd their G-d from that day and forward. Then the Gentiles shall know that because of their iniquity the house of Israel was exiled concerning which they betrayed Me and I hid My face from them and I gave them into the hand of their enemies..."* Ezekiel 39:21-23

This passage speaks clearly that it is indeed when the world sees how G-d deals with Israel and **not** the Church in the last days; that Israel will have a great influence on the Gentiles. However, in order for this wonderful message of the faithfulness of G-d to be demonstrated, and for both Jew and Gentile to be saved in that final hour, something must have had to take place. What is this? This is the re-establishment of the nation of Israel.

> *"Therefore thus says the L-rd G-d, 'Now I will return the captivity of Jacob and I will be merciful to all the house of Israel and I will be zealous for My holy Name...when I return them from the peoples and I will gather them from the land of their enemies and I will be sanctified in them before the eyes of many Gentiles. And they shall know that I am the L-rd their G-d in that I exiled them to the nations and I caused them to enter their own land and I will not leave any of them there. And I will not again hide My face from them when I poured out My Spirit upon the house of Israel, declares the L-rd G-d."* Ezekiel 39:25, 27-29

These verses make it impossible to embrace Replacement theology and to faithfully exegete the Word of G-d. This is why such theologians must forego standard hermeneutical principles and allegorize or ignore much of the Prophets in order to arrive at their perspectives which are so strongly anti-Israel. Based upon these verses, how can one not see G-d's hand in the return of six million Jews to their Biblical homeland in the last sixty years? Why is it that Replacement theologians are so enamored with the prospect of a Palestinian state when Ezekiel says time after time throughout his prophecy that G-d is going to return the descendants of Jacob to **their land**?

Once again, those who attempt to say it is the Church who fulfills these prophecies meet a theological wall, because it is only after returning these Jews to the Land of Israel, that G-d pours out His Spirit upon them. If the Church is the true possessor of this prophecy and others that promise the same thing, how can the following text say?

"And I will not again hide My face from them when I poured out My Spirit upon the house of Israel, declares the L-rd G-d."

The individuals to whom this passage is referring are those who do not have the Holy Spirit until that day. Hence, if the Church is "Israel", and it is the Church who inherits the land and not the natural descendants of Jacob, then those who are returned to the Land of Israel would be believers and the idea of G-d hiding His face and pouring out His Spirit, would not have any logical interpretation. Only for those who were not previously redeemed would such promises have relevance.

To those who attempt to divert the relevancy of Ezekiel's prophecy of Gog and Magog and assert that it speaks to a period of time which has already been fulfilled, I offer the following observations. First, the text specifically states it is for the end times (See Ezekiel 38:8, 16). Second, when have all the nations gone up to Israel to make war and the end results were both Jew and Gentile getting saved and the Holy Spirit being poured out? Third, when has Israel won a war because the L-rd punished his enemy by having it rain fire and sulfur (See Ezekiel 38:21-23)? Fourth, when did the inhabitants of Israel use the weaponry of their enemies for fuel for seven years (See Ezekiel 39:9-10)? Fifth, when did all the people of Israel spend seven months burying those who died in a war (See Ezekiel 39:11-16)? The response I always receive from the Replacement theologians when I confront them with these questions is that these things which Ezekiel speaks of cannot be taken at face value, for they are symbolic and must be allegorized.

Armageddon

Even though the battle of Armageddon and the War of Gog and Magog are the same event, it is helpful to examine some additional Scriptures which relate specifically to Armageddon. First, it is important for the reader to remember that when John mentions Armageddon in the book of Revelation, he states that the word is derived from the Hebrew language. The term "Armageddon" actually comes from two Hebrew words. The first part of **Ar**mageddon is the Hebrew word "Har", which means a mountain. The second part of Ar**mageddon** is from the Hebrew word which means "to tell" or "to proclaim". Hence, when referring to Armageddon in Hebrew, it is called Har Megiddo, which means the "mountain of His proclamation" or the "mountain of His messenger". Both possibilities offer some interesting background. The second word, which is translated "proclamation" or "telling", is the same word that is used for the booklet that guides a Jewish family through the sacred Passover meal. The booklet is called a "Hagaddah" and its purpose is to help the family fulfill the Biblical commandment of telling the story of Passover (Exodus 12:25-28); that is, proclaiming the message and the means of redemption. Is it not like G-d to deliver Israel from her enemy and to redeem His people in a place named "the mountain of His proclamation"?

The second rendering, "mountain of His messenger", is also a very appropriate name for this place. The term "magid" is very well-known among religious Jews because of a famous writing in Judaism called the Shulchan Aruch. This multi-volume work serves as a basis for understanding Jewish law. It was written in the 16th century by Rabbi Yosef Karo, who spoke repeatedly of being visited by an angel he called "hamagid", "the messenger".

Har Megiddo is well known throughout the history of the Holy Land. It was the site of many previous battles. Its location is most strategic, as it is situated at an ancient and modern intersection. Har Megiddo is nestled in the Jezreel Valley, at the end of the Carmel mountain range, and the beginning of the hill country of Samaria. Its importance cannot be over emphasized, for if an army wanted to attack Israel from the North, it would most certainly have to pass the Megiddo junction in order to travel along the Mediterranean coast and ascend to Jerusalem from the West. In fact, Har Megiddo would be the final place where an army could be stopped, as after Har Megiddo there is not another fitting location where the armies of Israel could mount a battle against an invading army prior to Jerusalem.

One should not forget that prospects of such a battle being won by Israel would be non-existent from a human standpoint. Nuclear weapons could not be utilized within these close proximities to Israel's citizens. A conventional war would leave the Israeli army absolutely outmatched by the fact that over and over the Prophets declare that Israel's enemy will be a coalition of all the nations in the world. Israel's only hope is the ancient promise of the Messiah. It is this very promise which will indeed be fulfilled at Har Megiddo.

Armageddon and the book of Revelation

We began our discussion of Armageddon in Revelation 16. When the sixth angel poured out his bowl, several significant things happened. The drying up of the Euphrates River provided a way for the kings of the East to travel towards Israel. There is an inherent relationship between these kings and demonic activity. The reader is told that unclean spirits, i.e. demons, come out of the mouth of the dragon, the beast, and the false prophet (See Revelation 16:13). This verse makes it clear that all the major players in this final empire are satanic in nature. These demons are said to come out of the mouth, in order to emphasize that by deception the world united with them against the L-rd's plan and

His people. It was through satanic inspiration that miracles were performed which also provided the basis for the world embracing the beast and following its leadership.

Although it is said that the kings of the East travel towards Israel for the purpose of making war, later on in this section one reads that this spiritual deception also captures the entire world,

"...which goes forth unto the kings of the earth and the whole world, to gather them for war...." Revelation 16:14

To where are these kings, who represent all the nations of the earth and their armies, being gathered? They are coming to Armageddon, the mountain where the L-rd will make a great proclamation concerning Who He is and who are His people. Israel, a small nation to begin with, will be totally outmatched when all the armies of the world stream into this tiny country from the north. It is likely that despite being outnumbered, the Israel Defense Forces will nevertheless attempt to defend her borders. There were historically, and remain today, places which are strategic and would offer the Israeli army the greatest likelihood of stopping an invading army; places like Hazor and Beth She'an. Because these places lie at crossroads between mountain ranges and the high ground, without question, Israel would mount defensive attacks from these places. However, because of the vast amount of soldiers and resources that an army which is a coalition from every nation in the world would possess, Israel's efforts will be certainly most ineffective. One can imagine the disappointment of Israel's citizens when they hear how quickly this invading army passes through Hazor and then Beth She'an. A prevalent feeling of utter hopelessness will cease the nation of Israel and its army as this massive army moves southwest toward Har Megiddo. The Israel Defense Forces will move all of its depleted resources to Har Megiddo, and citizens will also gather there in order to make one last defense of Jerusalem. Every Jew will know inwardly that the battle of Har Megiddo will be futile. This "last stand" will be based more in an unwillingness to surrender than any hope or thought of a victory.

Soldiers and armed citizens will know that Har Megiddo is where they will die.

If one has read the book of Revelation, then an entirely different expectation would be his. Here lies the problem; the vast majority of Jewish individuals have never read the book of Revelation. A few may have heard of the term "Armageddon", and know it has some connection with Christianity and the end times, but they would not associate it with Har Megiddo. In other words, there would not be any expectation that the battle which had been prophesied as Israel's greatest victory would be what was about to happen. There would no association of this battle with the prophecy of Zechariah either.

Zechariah Chapter 12 and Armageddon

In this section we will look at the Prophet's message to see what he says concerning this final battle which will happen at Har Megiddo. The first verse of Zechariah chapter 12 says,

"The burden of the word of the L-rd concerning Israel..."

The entire chapter speaks of a difficult time for Israel which will be caused by all the nations of the world. The term "burden of the L-rd" simply reveals that this difficult period for Israel is part of G-d's redemptive work in the last days. The source of this burden is all the nations of the world coming against the Jewish people in their attempt to wage war and capture Jerusalem. However, Zechariah reveals it will actually be those nations that will ultimately suffer G-d's judgment.

Zechariah 12:1 continues with remembering G-d as the Creator of the world:

"...He stretches out the heavens and establishes the earth and forms the spirit of man within him."

This verse utilizes language similar to the language for the creation of the world. However, the context for most of the book of Zechariah, especially the latter chapters, is the events which will bring about world redemption. Zechariah employs phrases relating to creation because redemption will bring about transformative changes to the world. Jerusalem is the focus of Zechariah 12:2 and serves to inform the reader that Jerusalem is foundational in G-d's plan to bring redemption to the world:

"Behold I am making Jerusalem a cup of poison for all the peoples around and also concerning Judah there will be a siege of Jerusalem." Zechariah 12:2

Zechariah 14:2 gives insight to what chapter 12 is referring—a war for Jerusalem.

"Behold the day of the L-rd is coming...and I (the L-rd) *will gather all the nations against Jerusalem for war..."*
Zechariah 14: 1-2

Zechariah 14:2 also states that all nations will join to make war and attack Jerusalem. Zechariah 12:2 calls Jerusalem a "cup of poison". There is actually another possible meaning for the Hebrew word translated "cup". It can also mean a "threshold". The point is that not only will those who attack Jerusalem be as those who drink poison, but attacking Jerusalem is like crossing a line that defines one's allegiance; that is, whether one is part of G-d's family or is G-d's enemy. The next verse describes Jerusalem as a heavy stone that will crush those who try to move it:

"And it shall come about on that day that I will make Jerusalem a burdensome stone to all the people, to all who burden her (Jerusalem); *they will cut* (themselves) *and all the nations of the earth shall be gathered unto her* (Jerusalem)."
Zechariah 12:3

Not only will those nations who attack Jerusalem be crushed, but the nations will actually be cut to pieces by doing so. The phrase "they will cut themselves" may have an additional meaning as well. There are other instances in the Bible which describe this cutting as a pagan practice related to the worship of a false god or as an expression of mourning and deep sorrow. This is similar to the practice in Judaism of "Kriah"—cutting or tearing one's garment as a sign of remorse or mourning for close relatives. Hence, Zechariah may be saying that those nations who attack Jerusalem in the last days are driven by a false god, and eventually they will realize their mistake and express deep sorrow and remorse.

In describing the war which will take place for Jerusalem, Zechariah reveals that G-d will intervene in a miraculous manner by striking the horses with blindness and their riders with madness. This may allude to causing the enemy's military armament to malfunction and those who operate it to act irrationally. Zechariah 12:4 also contains a most interesting statement:

> "*On that day says the L-rd, I will strike every horse with madness and its rider with craziness **and concerning the House of Judah I will open My eyes** and every horse of the peoples* (gentile nations) *I will strike with blindness.*"
>
> Zechariah 12:4

What is the significance of the phrase, "and concerning the House of Judah I (G-d) will open My eyes"? Israel has been in exile since the destruction of the Second Temple and, even though one can see G-d's hand moving in the life of the Jewish people in the establishment of the modern State of Israel and providing victory in the War of Independence, The Six Days War, and Yom Kippur War, G-d will move in the last days to deliver the Jewish people in a mighty and profound way. He will bring redemption and establish His Kingdom in such a great way that it will seem as though G-d's eyes were shut to the plight of His people for the last 2000 plus years.

In Zechariah 12:5-8, we see G-d strengthening the Jewish people and Jerusalem returning to its former status of glory which will greatly exceed her former splendor. Although G-d does indeed make Israel like fire and her enemies like straw, G-d Himself will defend His people in a personal way:

"And the leaders of Judah will say in their hearts, the inhabitants of Jerusalem (will also say) *my strength is in the L-rd of Hosts* (Who is) *their G-d. On that day I will make the leaders of Judah as a basis of fire against the trees and as a torch of fire against sheaves; and they will devour to the right and to the left—all the peoples round and Jerusalem will sit once more in her place in Jerusalem. The L-rd will save the tents of Judah as in the former times, so that the splendor of the house of David and the inhabitant of Jerusalem shall not exceed Judah. On that day the L-rd will defend the inhabitant of Jerusalem and it shall be that the failure* (the weak one) *among them on that day* (shall be) *like David and the house of David* (shall be) *as G-d—even as the Angel of the L-rd is before them."* Zechariah 12:5-8

It is also most clear from the following verse, that all the nations who will join together in opposition to Messiah's plan of establishing Jerusalem as the capital city for His Kingdom will be defeated:

"And it shall come about on that day I (the L-rd) *will seek to destroy all the nations coming against Jerusalem."*
Zechariah 12:9

The Hebrew word translated "destroy" in Zechariah 12:9 is a powerful word which describes an utter annihilation; it is basically the fulfillment of what G-d promised Abraham in Genesis chapter 12:

"I will bless those who bless you, but curse those who curse you..." Genesis 12:3

Those nations who will come to make war against Jerusalem will ultimately find themselves fighting against the Living G-d. Because they will be committing open rebellion and enmity toward G-d, their fate will be utter destruction. In the end-time battle for Jerusalem, the people of Israel will go through a dark and difficult hour, but through it the L-rd will bring about a significant spiritual change in them. Zechariah 12:10 reveals that G-d will pour out His Spirit on a certain group of the Jewish people in that time and reveal the One whom the Gemara (the major section of the Talmud) calls Messiah Ben Yoseph:

> *"I will pour out upon the House of David and upon the inhabitant of Jerusalem the spirit of grace and supplication and they will look upon Me Whom they have pierced and they will lament Him as the lamentation for a firstborn son and the bitterness for Him is as the bitterness for* (the death) *a firstborn son."* Zechariah 12:10

There are two groups of people mentioned in this verse: the House of David and the inhabitants of Jerusalem. To who is being referred by these descriptions? The "House of David" refers to those who have faith in G-d's promises to send a Redeemer in the last days. It is clear that the first part of Zechariah 12:10 is describing the same event as Isaiah 59:20-21:

> *"And a Redeemer shall come to Zion and to those who repent* (from) *sin of Jacob says the L-rd. And this is My covenant with them said the L-rd, My spirit* (will be) *upon you...."*
> Isaiah 59:20-21

In the last days G-d will move in a unique and powerful manner and will pour out His Spirit upon those who repent of sin. When Zechariah mentions "the Spirit of grace and supplication", to what is he referring? The word translated from the Hebrew as "grace" is similar in meaning to the words "mercy" or "forgiveness". There is, however, one important difference. The Hebrew word translated "grace" has a specific purpose attached to it. This purpose is to establish a bond or a relationship. Notice that Isaiah uses the word "covenant" in Isaiah 59:20-21. The prophet is reminding us of G-d's ultimate goal for redemption: His desire to enter into a new covenant relationship with the Jewish people. To this end He will pour out His grace upon them. The Hebrew word translated "supplication" is derived from the same word as grace. Hence, this verse in Isaiah also shows us that not only does G-d provide what is necessary to forgive the people of their sin (mercy), but He does so because of His great desire to have a new covenant relationship with them and even creates in them the desire (the spirit of supplication) to have such a relationship with Him.

As previously stated, the phrase "House of David" refers to those who have faith in a coming Messiah. The term "the inhabitant of Jerusalem" speaks about those who will inherit redemption. In essence, the terms "House of David" and "inhabitant of Jerusalem" are not speaking about two distinct groups of people, but revealing two aspects concerning these individuals. Because the term "David" refers to the promise of redemption that G-d made to David concerning Messiah, "The House of David" speaks of those who will be redeemed and thereby given the right to enter into the Messianic Kingdom. The term "inhabitant of Jerusalem" speaks of those who will inherit the full outcome of redemption with all the rights and privileges pertaining to it. How can this be derived from the term "inhabitant of Jerusalem"? Obviously, the word inhabitant refers to one dwelling in or connected to a place. Hence, the "inhabitant of Jerusalem" speaks of one who is connected to Jerusalem. The key to understanding this term is found in the meaning of the word Jerusalem. Jerusalem is composed of two Hebrew words, the first meaning "to possess" and the second meaning "peace". Hence Jerusalem speaks of those who will possess peace. The term peace does not speak necessarily of a situation absent of conflict and wars, but rather the term shalom (peace) is derived from a word which means "to complete" or "to fulfill". For example, in Modern Hebrew if one has a debt, he must fulfill his obligation, that is to complete that which is lacking. When he pays his debt, he is making peace. In fact, the Modern Hebrew word for "to pay" is derived from this same word from which "peace/shalom" comes. Therefore, the term "Jerusalem" means "those who possess the completion or the fulfillment of G-d's will". What is it that G-d desires? One only needs to return to the book of Genesis to find in chapter 12 that G-d's purpose for bringing Israel into existence was to use the Jewish people as an instrument to bless all the families of the earth. (See Genesis 12:3).

The second half of Zechariah 12:10 deals with the means by which these things are accomplished, i.e. the fulfillment of redemption. When the text says, "*They will look upon Me...*", to who is the text referring? It is clear from the context that G-d is speaking because He speaks in first person about pouring out His Spirit. Interestingly, among Jewish and Christian commentators there is a consensus that Zechariah 12:10 refers to the Messiah.

Judaism teaches that there are two Messiahs: Messiah Ben David and Messiah Ben Yoseph. Messiah Ben David is the Messiah who will defeat the enemies of Israel and bring about the kingdom of G-d. Messiah Ben Yoseph is seen as an assistant to Messiah Ben David and One who suffers. Some have stated that it is Messiah Ben Yoseph to whom the suffering servant passages in the latter chapters of Isaiah speak. The Talmud (Gemara, Meseket Sukah) says that the Messiah who appears in Zechariah 12:10 is Messiah Ben Yoseph. Hence this section of the Gemara is calling one to interpret Zechariah 12:10 as a lamentation for the Messiah called Ben Yoseph who was killed previously (See Meseket Sukah 52a). Such an interpretation poses a serious conflict for Judaism. It is clear from Zechariah 12:9 that G-d defeats those who will wage war against Jerusalem and the Jewish people at the end of the age. Rambam, the famous Jewish commentator of both Jewish law and the Bible, offers a view which is embraced by Judaism as a whole. This view is that Messiah Ben David will fight Israel's enemies at the end of this age and bring about the final redemption. Therefore, it is problematic to assert that Zechariah 12:10 is speaking of Messiah Ben Yoseph instead of Messiah Ben David, according to the Talmud and the prevailing opinion in Judaism.

The fact that the "House of David" is mentioned in Zechariah 12:10 also hints that what is being done in this section of Zechariah is the work of Messiah Ben David. The reason that there is a desire among the rabbis to interpret the subject of Zechariah 12:10 as Messiah Ben Yoseph is because the verse says he was stabbed/pierced. Both Jewish and Christian commentators interpret the wounds mentioned in Zechariah 12:10 as relating to Messiah's death, that is, Messiah Ben Yoseph's death according to Judaism. The problem is that the One Who will bring Israel victory in the last days is Messiah Ben David according to all views. Hence, what about the wounds that Zechariah 12:10 mentions? These are the wounds that belong to Messiah Ben Yoseph.

Let us restate the problem. The Talmud says the subject of Zechariah 12:10 is Messiah Ben Yoseph, the suffering servant. However, the work that is being done in this section is clearly the work of Messiah Ben David (fighting Israel's enemies and establishing His kingdom on earth). Hence, both Messiahs of the Jewish tradition are alluded to in this section, but only one Messiah is present. This poses an irreconcilable dilemma for Judaism. There is, however, a simple solution. There are not two Messiahs, but only one. This one Messiah has two distinct roles which He will accomplish at two distinct times. His first role is to accomplish the work of redemption for the world, and the second is to bring about the actual results of the work of redemption to Israel and the world; that is, the Kingdom of G-d. Zechariah chapter three offers an interesting illustration which helps the reader understand the nature of Messiah's work of redemption.

In chapter three the prophet Zechariah has a vision of Joshua the high priest standing before the Angel of the L-rd with Satan standing on his right side to accuse him. As high priest, Joshua represents the whole house of Israel. Joshua stands before the L-rd clothed in soiled garments which represent the sins of the Jewish people. As Joshua stands there, the L-rd commands that his soiled garments be removed, representing the removal of sins. This is the work of redemption:

"And He (the L-rd) *answered and said to the ones standing before Him saying, 'remove the soiled garments from upon him and clothe him with the festival garments".*

Zechariah 3:4

It is Messiah's role to pay the price of redemption for all mankind, Jew and Gentile alike. It is significant that later on in this heavenly scene, Zechariah 3:8 mentions *"My Servant* (the) *Branch"*. All commentators connect this phrase to the Messiah. Zechariah 3:9 then goes on to say:

"...I will remove the sin of that land in one day."

Zechariah 3:9

The verse reveals that in one day G-d will do the work necessary to redeem Israel and the world. Furthermore, the fact that the vision speaks of Joshua being clothed with soiled garments and then clean ones teaches a vicarious sacrifice. Because the high priest represents Israel before G-d, his soiled garments represent sin and his clean garments represent Israel's new status by means of the redemptive work of Messiah. It is Messiah, as we have discussed, Who does the work of Messiah Ben Yoseph and suffers for the sins of Israel and the world. In this passage, Joshua the high priest is faced with the message of Messiah Who became sin for us so that His righteousness might be upon all those who receive Him personally. This is also the message of the well-known 53rd chapter of Isaiah. The type of sacrifice the high priest makes for Israel on the Day of Atonement is vicarious: that is, the sins of the people he confesses upon the goat which then suffers the outcome of sin (death) while the people are forgiven. Zechariah chapter 3 reveals exactly that. One can read much more in depth about the vicarious sacrifice of Yom Kippur in Leviticus 16.

Similar to Zechariah 3:9, Messiah's work of redemption, i.e. His substitutionary sacrifice for the sins of Israel, was achieved in one day. Such a view is quite different from what Judaism commonly teaches today—that Israel will merit her own redemption by doing good deeds. This was the teaching of the late Lubavitcher Rebbe who said that a certain number of good deeds must be done prior to Messiah being revealed, and therefore he encouraged people to do good deeds saying that "perhaps the good deed that you do will be the one that brings the final redemption." Zechariah three paints a different picture of redemption. It is clear that Israel cannot make itself clean, that it is not by merit that Israel will be redeemed, but by the sovereign plan of G-d Who will simply give Messiah the word to complete the work of redemption on behalf of the people.

In returning to Zechariah 12:10, one observes a key piece of information. When the Messiah, Who has been pierced / stabbed appears, people will see Him and lament for Him. The verse, in fact, presents the image of a very unique lamentation:

"I will pour out upon the House of David and upon the inhabitant of Jerusalem the spirit of grace and supplication and they will look upon Me whom they have pierced and they will lament Him as the lamentation for a firstborn son and the bitterness for Him is as the bitterness for (the death) *a firstborn son." Zechariah 12:10*

In Judaism, when one mourns the death of a close family member, such as a son, a thirty-day mourning period is observed. It's clear that Zechariah is referring to this thirty-day mourning period.

There is something very unique about Israel's mourning the Messiah when He returns to deliver Israel from the nations which will gather against Jerusalem. This mourning is significant and reveals a vital clue concerning the identity of Messiah. Zechariah 12:11 says:

"On that day the mourning in Jerusalem will be great as the mourning of Hadad-Rimmon in the valley of Megiddo (Har Megiddo or **Armageddon**).*"*

What is the significance of this verse? The Talmud says in Meseket Moed Kattan 28b that this verse alludes to two events. The first event is the death of King Ahab at the hand of whom the Gemara calls Hadad-Rimmon (see I Kings 22). The second event to which it refers is the death of King Josiah, who was slain in the valley of Megiddo (see II Chronicles 35). What is important about this citation from the Talmud is that both references refer to two men, Ahab and Josiah, who both made a tragic mistake which cost them their lives. Why does the Talmud impose these interpretations upon the verse within the context of Messiah's coming? Whether or not the Talmud intended to do so or not is unknown, but such an interpretation provides a basis for a proper interpretation of Zechariah 12:11 that fits nicely into the reality of this situation. The Talmudic view means that when Messiah comes, i.e. returns, Israel will also be convicted by the reality that she also committed a tragic error by not recognizing Yeshua as her Messiah. This time when Messiah returns and Israel sees His wounds, her people will recognize His identity and mourn His death which the nation did not do when He laid down His life to make redemption on Passover nearly 2,000 years ago.

When one understands the relationship between Zechariah chapter 12 and Armageddon, he understands why Israel will feel hopeless and believe the nation is about to be destroyed. Yet, in the midst of this time, Messiah will come and fulfill His promise. Quite a picture is being presented here. Israel is gallantly making a last stand. She has been badly beaten in her attempts to stop the massive invading army previously losing countess soldiers. She is grossly outnumbered and does not have any allies. There is no one to turn to for help. Finally, realizing her utter hopeless through physical means, she turns to G-d in prayer. What will be the outcome of this prayer?

Revelation 16:17-18:24

This section begins with the seventh angel pouring out the final bowl. He poured it into the air and as a result, a voice was heard coming from the heavenly Temple. The voice proclaimed, "It is done!" Obviously this message refers to the victory Messiah's return brought for Israel over the beast and all the nations of the world which were loyal to this empire. Although the victory has been announced, there are still events which must happen in order for this conflict to be brought to its conclusion. The purpose, however, of this proclamation is to foreshadow the transition away from the beast's rule, to that of Messiah's reign. Once again, when the book of Revelation wants to signal a significant change, one reads the familiar verse,

"And it came about voices and thunder and lightning and a great earthquake; which has not happened since men were upon the earth, so great of earthquake, so great!"

Revelation 16:18

Although this verse appears several other times in the book of Revelation, this time the earthquake is spoken of in a unique manner. Babylon, the term which relates to the center of the beast's empire, was divided and the cities of the nations fell. The reader is further told that Babylon was remembered by G-d and that He will give to her the cup which contains the anger of His wrath. The judgment of this seventh bowl is great hail from heaven which fell upon man and, once again, instead of seeking mercy and repenting, men blasphemed G-d because of the great severity of the plague of hail.

The next chapter of the book of Revelation, chapter 17, has been studied previously when discussing the beast (See chapter five). Not only does it offer additional information in identifying and understanding the beast, it also provides the basis for comprehending the "great harlot". Revelation chapter 18 also proclaims the beast's defeat and offers a warning to the reader not to have any connection with the beast and the great harlot. The chapter ends with a statement that in Babylon was found the blood of both the Prophets and the saints who were slain by the beast (See Revelation 18:24). Not only does this verse demonstrate a connection between the Prophets and believers, but should also be understood as an admonition to believers to study fervently the message of the Prophets so that each one will be ready and stand faithfully in the last days.

Chapter 11

"The Second Coming"

Revelation chapter 19 contains a vision of Messiah Yeshua returning to earth in order to establish His Kingdom. We have learned from the previous chapter that His return will happen during the end of a great period of tribulation for Israel. Not only will Israel be suffering as a result of the beast, so also will the rest of the world; first as a result of G-d's judgment and then His wrath. Two primary sections of Scripture will be examined in this chapter; first, Revelation chapter 19 and the opening verses of chapter 20 and then later, portions of Matthew chapter 24.

Throughout this period of judgment and wrath, the Bible emphasizes the refusal of the world to repent. Instead of seeking G-d's mercy by means of the Gospel, over and over the people blaspheme G-d. This is in strong contrast to the opening verse of Revelation chapter 19,

> "*And after these things I heard a great voice of a large crowd in the heavens saying, 'Halleluiah, salvation and glory and honor and power to the L-rd our G-d.*"

This verse is very similar to Daniel 7:14, which speaks also of Messiah's coming. The reason for this adoration for G-d is because He has judged the world and avenged His servants. There is a clear emphasis on worship in this chapter in order to remind the reader that it is only Messiah Who can create a people capable of worshiping the Living G-d. One also reads that the smoke from the judgment placed upon the great harlot will rise forever. This detail attests to the fact that G-d's punishment for those who reject His plan and purposes is eternal.

The 24 elders are again mentioned, showing again the unity that has now been established between Israel and the believers. This was achieved when Israel saw that the One Who delivered her at Armageddon was, in fact, Yeshua of Nazareth. Not only do these elders worship in heaven, but a call goes forth from the Throne of G-d for all to worship Him, both great and small (See Revelation 19:4-6). Kingdom worship will be initiated by a very special event known as the marriage banquet of the Lamb. Prior to Messiah's coming to this banquet, His bride, i.e. believers, will have had to make herself ready.

> *"And it was given to her in order that she be clothed with byssus*, clean and magnificent; for the byssus is the righteousness of the saints."* Revelation 19:8

> ***Byssus is a type of fine cotton that was highly prized by the ancients. It is also mentioned in Luke 16:19 and is usually translated in most English translations as "fine linen".**

Within this passage, John sees an angel (messenger) from heaven who is communicating to him these truths. In addition, the messenger instructs him to write that those who are part of the family of God are those individuals who have the testimony of Messiah Yeshua which he states is the spirit of prophecy. He unites this fact with an admonition to worship G-d (See Revelation 19:9-10). It is immediately after these things heaven was opened and a white horse appeared with One sitting upon it. This is in contrast to the first seal of Revelation chapter 6, where a counterfeit messiah was seen. It is most significant that the real Messiah is called Faithful and True.

Although Yeshua is gracious and forgiving, what is emphasized at His Second Coming is the fact that He judges sin and makes war. These two aspects are what manifest His righteousness. A G-d Who makes war and will place wrath upon the world is very difficult for many people to accept. They might say such a G-d is not the One Who they know. They would be absolutely right, for all too often people's understanding of G-d originates from their own human reason. In other words, their "god" is nothing more than what their own human intellect, along with things they may have read or heard, have created. It is most insightful when the

True Messiah appears that the reader is told that He has a name which no man knows (See Revelation 19:12). No sooner than stating this, the reader is told that His name is the WORD OF G-D. This passage's purpose is to inform and teach all of mankind that the only way which one can come to know the true G-d and His Messiah is according to the revelation which is contained in the Holy Scriptures.

Even though the reader of the book of Revelation has already been given a glimpse of the destruction of the beast and its followers, now with the coming of Messiah this victory is revisited. In this vision of Messiah's coming to destroy the enemies of Israel at Armageddon, the reader is told He is not alone. The armies of heaven come with Him, also riding upon white horses. Those who are in the army are clothed with the similar white, clean byssus. The only difference between the garments of the saints and those in the army is one of the adjectives which describes the garments. For the saints, a word is used that means "bright" or having a great "splendor", while for those in the army a word which means "white" appears. Some have suggested that the similarities are to show that the two groups are, in fact, the same individuals and the use of a different adjective should not necessarily be understood as providing a basis for understanding that the text is referring to two different groups. If, in fact, the saints are also those who make up the army, it would agree with Yeshua's statement,

"...in order that where I am, you also shall be." John 14:3

When Yeshua returns, He will have a sharp sword which goes forth from His mouth. It is with this sword that He will destroy the beast, the kings of the earth, those in their armies, and those who received the mark of the beast (See Revelation 19:15-20). This sword may, in fact, be a symbolic reference to the Gospel (See Matthew 10:34), for it is actually the rejection of the Gospel that brought about their destruction.

The battle of Armageddon ends with the beast and the false prophet being seized and cast alive into the lake which burns with fire and brimstone. It is only when one arrives at Revelation chapter 20 that he learns that also the Devil, i.e. Satan, is bound and cast into the Abyss for a thousand years. Why a thousand years? What will take place on earth during this time? These questions and many more will be dealt with in the next chapter of this book. However, for now, the latter section of Matthew chapter 24 will be examined in order to provide a greater understanding of Messiah's Second Coming.

Matthew 24 and the Second Coming

It has already been discussed that this chapter deals with questions concerning the end times. Yeshua's disciples asked two important questions, "What is the sign of Your coming? And, what is the sign of the end of the world" (See Matthew 24:3)? In regard to the second question, it is clear that the disciples are referring to the establishment of the Kingdom. Because Judaism then and now associates the Kingdom with the coming of the Messiah, it is significant that this text separates them. The issue which must be examined is whether the reference to Yeshua's coming could, in fact, be the Rapture. Before Yeshua deals directly with these questions, He points out as previously discussed, that there will be a period of calamities which will affect the world (See Matthew 24:6-8) and then believers will be persecuted. All of this will provide an opportunity for the Gospel to be preached in the world (See Matthew 24:9-14). This persecution will end after the Abomination of Desolation (See Matthew 24:15), when Israel and the Jewish people in general, will go through the most difficult time of persecution in the history of humanity (See Matthew 24:16-26 and Daniel 12:1).

In the midst of this section, it is difficult to know exactly where Yeshua concludes speaking about the time period known as Jacob's Trouble and returns to speaking to the disciples concerning events which will impact believers. A possible explanation for this difficulty is that believers will be suffering intense persecution prior to the Rapture as will also Israel prior to the Second Coming. Due to this, both groups will be looking for the promise of Messiah's deliverance. Even though this section may have relevance for both groups, I suggest that verses 16-31 speak primarily to Israel and the Jewish people, rather than believers in Yeshua. It is absolutely for certain that verses 29-31 are addressing the Second Coming and not the Rapture. This is because the moon is said not to give off any light and the sun has been darkened, whereas prior to the Rapture the moon will be red like blood (See Joel 3:3, 2:31 English, and Revelation 6:12). In the next verse one reads,

"And at that time will be manifested the sign of the Son of Man in heaven; and at that time all the tribes of the earth will lament/mourn, and they will see the Son of Man coming upon the clouds of heaven with great power and glory."
Matthew 24:30

This verse is no doubt based upon Daniel 7:13 and Zechariah 12:10. There is no way to interpret this statement other than referring to the time period after Jacob's Trouble. Although the mentioning of clouds could apply likewise to the Rapture, the reference to lamentation or mourning could only apply to the Second Coming. Special attention must be given to a few significant elements found in this verse. First, the reader is told that all the tribes of the earth will lament/mourn. This verse does not only relate to Israel or just the Jewish people, but all individuals regardless of ethnicity. Second, the verb which the writer of this verse was inspired to select. The Greek word can mean "to lament" something that is undesirable to one or it can mean "to mourn" as in a response to a person's death. It is precisely the dual meaning of this word which fits the full context of the verse.

When Jewish individuals will see Messiah coming to deliver them from the nations of the world, they will recognize that all the while the One Who by and large the Jewish community spoke against is, in fact, their Redeemer. Having not responded properly to His first coming and the death He died as a propitiation for sin, this time the world Jewry will mourn for Yeshua and receive Him and His Gospel. While this great day of national salvation is occurring for Israel, the nations will lament Yeshua's return, as He will wage war against them and destroy all but a remnant of them.

In keeping with many prophecies and the *Amidah* prayer of Judaism, the Messiah will gather up Jewish individuals (by means of angels) wherever they may be and bring them to Israel.

> *"And He sends forth His angels with the blowing of the great shofar and they will gather together His elect from the four winds, from the ends of heaven unto their ends."*
>
> Matthew 24:31

Notice how similar this verse from the New Testament is to the blessing in the Shemona Ezreh entitled "Gathering the exiles",

> *"Sound the great shofar for our freedom, and lift up the miraculous banner to gather our exiles; and gather us together from the four corners of the earth to our land. Blessed are You O L-rd, the One Who gathers the dispersed ones of His people Israel."*

In the next section of Matthew 24, it is clear that Yeshua is addressing all readers, including His future disciples. His instructions in verse 32 are highly problematic for those who incorrectly assert that there is no longer any special prophetic significance attached to Israel. The "fig tree" is a well-known reference to Israel; therefore believers should pay great attention, especially in the last days, to what is taking place in the Land of Israel. In this section Yeshua states,

> *"And from the fig tree, learn the parable, now whenever her branch becomes tender and the leaves should generate; you know that near is the summer. And so you, whenever you*

should see all these things, you will know that it is near—at
the door." Matthew 24:32-33

Not only should one pay attention to what is happening to the
Jewish people and the nation of Israel, a person needs to form his
views based upon Scriptural insight. This is in opposition to a
growing numbers of "Christians" who want to strip away from
Israel any unique status and form their opinions concerning the
conflict in the Middle East without using prophecy to guide them.
Of course it will be this opposition to the modern State of Israel
which is a key indicator that G-d is at work and the end times are at
hand. It is precisely these unbiblical views against Israel that will
justify the coming persecution of the Jewish people and the State
of Israel which Matthew 24 places prior to the Second Coming.

There is no doubt that beginning in verse 32 and the "parable of
the fig tree", that Yeshua is addressing the questions of the
disciples in a general way. This is seen in the fact that twice
(verses 33 and 34) He uses the phrase *"all these things"*. In verse
36 Yeshua states,

> *"But concerning that day and the hour, no one knows..."*

To what event is Yeshua referring? There are two possible
answers to this question: the Rapture or the Second Coming. It is
the following section of Scripture which answers this question. In
this section Yeshua speaks about the days of Noah. Even though
from a moral and spiritual standpoint the time of Noah was very
displeasing to G-d, people ignored the L-rd's call to repent and
continued living in their "normal" manner. This is the intent of the
verses,

> *"And just as the days of Noah, thus will be also the coming of*
> *the Son of Man. For just as they in the days of Noah, the ones*
> *before the flood were eating and drinking, marrying and*
> *giving in marriage; until the day Noah entered into the ark,*
> *and they did not know until the flood came and took all; Thus*
> *will be also the coming of the Son of Man."*
> Matthew 24:37-39

The example is most informative in assisting the reader to understand which issue Messiah is addressing. The issue is the Rapture. This is because it is during the first half of the final seven year period, even though believers will be sharing the Gospel and speaking out against the policies of the beast and the false prophet, the world will be ignoring these things, much like the world ignored the call of Noah. Noah building a giant ark in the location he did certainly would have attracted the people's attention, but his calls to repentance went unheeded due to the fact that the world appeared to be in a normal state.

In regard to the end times, after the initial hardships that will come upon the world, "the beginning of sorrows" (Matthew 24:6-8), the beast will rise to power and solve the chaos that is plaguing the world. It is because of the stability which the beast will bring to the world that most individuals will pledge their loyalty to the beast. Only believers will oppose the unrighteous and unbiblical characteristics of this world empire. As the beast is persecuting believers, imprisoning them and killing them, the rest of the world will be carrying on with life, enjoying what will later prove to be a very temporary "peace" and "prosperity". It can only be during the first half of the final seven year period that life would be normal and there would be marriages etc., for in the second half such behavior would be impossible with first the judgment of G-d falling and then His wrath.

The aforementioned passage ends with the phrase, "*until the day Noah entered into the ark*". Here is a very important question, "Did Noah know, prior to the flood actually coming, when it was going to begin?" I am amazed by the number of people I have asked that the vast majority answer, "No". This is not what the Bible reveals, for it clearly states that,

> "*Then the L-rd said to Noah, 'You come and all your house to the ark, for you I have seen to be righteous before Me in this generation. For in seven more days I will cause it to rain upon the earth 40 days and 40 nights and I will blot out all existence which I have made from upon the earth.' On this*

very day Noah came and Shem and Ham and Japeth, the sons of Noah, and the wife of Noah, and the three wives of his sons with them to the ark. And they came...and the L-rd shut it (the door) *for them.*" Genesis 7:1, 4, 13, and 16

In a similar way, believers will know as the time approaches that the Rapture is at hand. The Scripture says we will not know the day or hour, but that it is imminent, we will know. However, for the rest of the world, they will be living without any thought that the blessed hope from the L-rd is about to happen, in the same way that the world was totally unaware that the flood was about to take place.

In this section Yeshua gives two additional examples concerning His coming. He speaks first about two individuals in the field and one being taken and one being left behind. Similarly, in the second example, there are two people at the mill and one is taken and one left behind. Critics have pointed out that if this is the Rapture, and the ones being taken are being taken to heaven and the ones being left behind are those who will experience G-d's judgment and wrath, as those in the days of Noah; then there is something that does not fit. They argue that in the example with Noah, it was those who were judged that were taken away, yet in the two examples which follow, those being taken away are the ones being delivered.

At first glance this seems to pose a difficult problem for those who assert that this section (Matthew 24:36-44) is referring to the Rapture. The similarity in language "being taken or took" is only similar in English. It is most significant that, in the two examples concerning the field and the mill, a different Greek word is used. In the passage dealing with the flood, the Greek word carries in this context a meaning of death and destruction; however, in the latter two examples, the Greek word which appears has to do with receiving a person to oneself. There is a degree of intimacy contained in this word. A well-known occurrence of this word is found in John 14:3.

*"And if I go and prepare for you a place, again I am coming and **will take** you to Myself; in order that where I am, also you will be."*

The fact that the same word is used in Matthew 24:40-41 and John 14:3, and that the context in both of these passages is Messiah fulfilling a promise to His followers, should lead the reader to conclude that the subject of Messiah in these two sections is indeed the Rapture.

Hence, both the Rapture and the Second Coming offer a message of hope and deliverance to believers (the Rapture) and Israel (Second Coming); yet there is a significant difference between them. Whereas the Rapture is a reward to the faithful, the Second Coming will manifest the faithfulness of G-d to Israel and thereby lead Israel to finally accept the Gospel of Yeshua, her deliverer. Matthew 24 concludes with several admonitions to watch and be ready for Messiah's coming. These statements can equally apply to the believer as well as Israel.

Chapter 12

"The Millennial Kingdom"

The fact that there are those who deny the Millennial Kingdom is not new. What is somewhat new is the popularity that this view is gaining by an increasing number of evangelicals. What lies at the heart of such a theological position? A desire to view Israel as a rebel nation and whom has broken G-d's covenant and having lost her status as the Chosen People of G-d. Those who interpret the Bible more literally are compelled by a wealth of prophecy to acknowledge that there is a time when Israel will obey her calling and be used by G-d as the leader of the world. When will Israel fulfill these prophecies and lead the world in worshiping Yeshua?

This time will be the thousand years when the Messiah is ruling from the earthly city of Jerusalem. It is the Millennial Kingdom which will be Israel's finest hour, as she will finally obey the L-rd and manifest to the nations why G-d has chosen Israel from all the other nations. In reality, G-d did not choose Israel from among the other nations, but Scripture reveals that G-d created a new people supernaturally, when He opened the womb of Sarah and gave her conception. It is vital for one to remember that according to the words of Paul, Isaac is the child of promise (Galatians 4:23). Although ultimately the Abrahamic covenant is fulfilled by Messiah Yeshua, this does not invalidate the fact that a chosen people would come physically from the loins of Abraham and that this people was given specific promises which must be fulfilled. It is the failure to recognize the validity of these prophecies which causes those who reject the reality of a Millennial Kingdom to be forced to attach the future obedience of Israel to believers and to fail to see a literal Kingdom where the Messiah rules from the earthly Jerusalem.

Those who deny the Millennial Kingdom (Amillennialists) are forced to do some "theological acrobatics" in their attempt to handle the clear teachings of Scripture which reveal a Kingdom full of justice and righteousness, having its origin in the earthy Jerusalem. The result for many Replacement theologians (a high percentage of Replacement theologians are Amillenialists) is to assert that the tribulation, which both Yeshua and the Prophets spoke of, is not unique to the last days; rather it has occurred throughout the Church age. Therefore it is not Messiah's return which defeats the enemies of G-d, but rather it is the successful preaching of the Gospel that establishes the kingdom of G-d. It is, therefore, their belief that Messiah does not return to establish the Kingdom; rather Yeshua takes His place in a Kingdom which has been prepared by the Church. Others combine the Scripture for the Millennial Kingdom and the New Jerusalem together and allow for a period of tribulation at the end of this age, but with Messiah's return, the final Kingdom, i.e. the New Jerusalem, is established. Both views see no special relevance for Israel (the land), nor the Jewish people today that is different from any other nation or people. Therefore, Replacement theologians understand that the promise of a re-gathering of Jewish people back to the Land of Israel is actually fulfilled by individuals, regardless of ethnicity, accepting Yeshua in the land that G-d promised to Abraham,

> *"On that day the L-rd made a covenant with Avram saying, 'To your descendants I have given this land from the river of Egypt unto the great river, the Euphrates River."*
>
> Genesis 15:18

I understand that Replacement theologians want to say that it is believers in Yeshua who are the rightful heirs of the Abrahamic covenant and therefore the ultimate heirs of the Kingdom. For them, the Land of Israel is spiritualized to equate to the Kingdom. The problem with this oversimplification of Scripture poses an irreconcilable problem. As has been previously stated several times, the way which G-d will deal with the Jewish people and the Land of Israel in the last days will be a testimony to the Gentiles and it is this testimony that will cause many of them to come to faith prior to Messiah's return. Part of what G-d will do which will testify to His faithfulness will be His returning the Jewish people to their historical homeland. If it is simply individuals who live in the lands between the two rivers previously mentioned coming to faith, where is the fulfillment of G-d returning His people from exile?

This is one small example of how numerous prophecies are ignored by Replacement theologians or how their spiritualization and allegorizing rip the various texts from their context. When one examines their explanations for the prophecies concerning Israel, these explanations run back and forth between two positions; either the prophecy had its fulfillment in the days of the prophets, or the prophecy must be applied to the church. This methodology is more related to a preconceived bias against the nation of Israel and the Jewish people, rather than in sound exegetical and hermeneutical methodology.

Satan and the Millennial Kingdom

For those theologians who assert that the Church age (from the resurrection or Pentecost to the Second coming) is the Millennial Kingdom, and that the Millennium should be rightly understood as a spiritual kingdom, the following two verses, which speak of Satan being bound offer quite a dilemma.

> "*And he seized the Dragon, the old serpent; which is the Devil and Satan and bound him a thousand years and cast him into the Abyss and shut it. He sealed it in order that he should not deceive the nations any longer, until the thousand years should be complete and afterwards it is necessary to release him a little while.*" Revelation 20:2-3

It is hard to believe that theologically trained individuals could believe that Satan is actually bound now and has been bound since the resurrection of Yeshua. In their view, it is Messiah's ascension which establishes the Millennial Kingdom. The problem is that it is not His ascension which brings the Kingdom, but according to Scripture, it is His descent from heaven which brings the Millennial Kingdom into existence. For those who believe that there is no Millennial Kingdom, they have no problem with the fact that at the return of Messiah, Satan is bound and the New Jerusalem is initiated immediately upon His return. The problem these theologians have is what to do with the part of the verse which says that Satan must be released for a little while? There is nothing which these theologians can offer as an explanation, based upon an exegetical basis, why after the New Jerusalem is established and perfection is achieved, Satan would be released. This is but one of numerous examples of how such theologians neglect many aspects contained in prophetic passages. Some have tried to solve this discrepancy by asserting that Satan is released at the beginning of the final seven year period. Such a view is impossible, because according to the book of Revelation, the tribulation which Satan causes is prior to Messiah's return which, in fact, initiates the Millennium. Furthermore, there have not been the types of tribulation that the book of Revelation describes during the Church age. The passage states that after Satan has been released from the Abyss, he goes out and deceives the nations, but the battle is most anticlimactic— nothing is said about any tribulation. Satan will simply deceive and gather a portion of the nations to make war, but prior to any action against the saints, Satan and his followers are destroyed in an instant.

Although Amillennialists and Postmillennialists have built theological doctrines that have gathered a great following, they must confess that their views of interpreting Scripture are far from literal. They also leave a great wealth of prophecies untouched and justify doing so by asserting that they are either too symbolic to understand, speak to an earlier period of time, or are fulfilled by believers. For those who believe,

> "All Scripture is inspired by G-d and is beneficial for doctrine, for reproof, for correction, for admonition in righteousness; in order that complete should be the man of G-d, for every good work having been equipped." II Timothy 3:16-17

The emphasis is that **all Scripture** is beneficial for doctrine. Hence, theological dogma which fails to include in its doctrine the entire revelation of G-d's Holy, Inspired, and Inerrant Word is a theology that should be avoided.

Understanding the Purpose of the Millennium

A Millennial Temple with sacrifices is just one of the prophetic realities that Amillennialists, Postmillennialists, and Replacement theologians fail to explain, unless saying that the Temple and sacrifices are only symbolic and spiritual is considered a sufficient explanation. In this section, a brief overview will be provided to assist one in understanding not only why there is a literal Millennial Kingdom, but what will take place in this Kingdom. It has already been stated that the Millennium will be Israel's finest hour. This is the case, not because as a Jewish individual this pleases me, rather because the Word of G-d reveals it. Isaiah prophesied that,

> *"And it shall come about in the end of days the mountain of the house of the L-rd shall be established, chief among the mountains and lifted up higher than hills and all nations shall stream unto it and many people will go and they shall say, 'Come and let us go up to the mountain of the L-rd, to the house of the G-d Jacob and He will teach us from His ways and we shall walk in His paths for from Zion shall go forth the Torah and the Word of the L-rd from Jerusalem. And He will judge among nations and reprove many peoples, and they shall beat their swords into shovels and their spears into pruning shears, nation will not lift up against nation a sword and they shall no longer learn warfare."* Isaiah 2:2-4

These verses speak about Millennial events which certainly have not taken place yet. A quick examination of what Isaiah states will prove helpful in understanding several of the foundational points related to the Millennium. First, the mountain of the L-rd must be established. To which mountain is the text referring? The fact that terms such as Jerusalem and Zion appear in this passage leaves little room for speculation. The house of our G-d is an obvious reference to the Temple. If, in fact, the Millennial Kingdom is here and now, since the ascension of the Messiah, clearly the statement Yeshua makes in Matthew 24 concerning the last days and the occurrence of an increase in warfare is highly problematic, with Isaiah's prophecy that nations will destroy their weapons and not learn warfare any more.

To those who state that the Millennial Kingdom and the New Jerusalem is one and the same, other problems are present. First, this passage states that there is a Temple (See Isaiah 2:3), but in the book of Revelation there is a verse which states that the New Jerusalem has no Temple (See Revelation 21:22). This verse states that the L-rd G-d Almighty and the Lamb is its Temple (please note the singular verb 'is" is utilized in the Greek, rather than the plural "are"; attesting to the unity between the L-rd and Messiah). Naturally, there will be those theologians who will want to spiritualize this passage and say the Temple in the Isaiah passage can be understood as intimacy with G-d and not an actual building. This allegorical interpretation seems to be hard to justify when one reviews the final nine chapters of Ezekiel's prophecy. In these chapters it is absolutely impossible to reconcile the description of the Temple area, the offerings which will be made at the altar, instructions to the Priest and Levites, and the division of the land, with the information provided in the book of Revelation concerning the New Jerusalem. There is simply no exegetical means for asserting that the Millennial Kingdom and the New Jerusalem are the same period.

The Scriptures do in fact provide the Bible student with enough information to rightly understand what will take place in the Millennium and why. First, one is able to identify who will be in the Millennial Kingdom and what will be each person's respective role. The Millennial Kingdom will be comprised of the following groups of people:

1. Those who came to faith in the Gospel (Jewish and Gentile) prior to the Rapture.
2. Those who came to faith in the Gospel (Jewish and Gentile) after the Rapture.
3. Those who are born during the Millennial Kingdom.

In regard to the first group, these individuals who had taken part in the Rapture will have received a new body and their respective role is to rule and reign with Messiah as Revelation 20:4 clearly states. In other words, believers will have a supervisory role. It is the second and third group that will make up the citizens of the Millennial Kingdom. A very important aspect of this Kingdom is that Israel will take a leadership role over the nations. One needs to be mindful of the basis for Israel's leadership. As Isaiah stated,

"For from Zion shall go forth the Torah and the Word of the L-rd from Jerusalem."

Israel will, in the Millennial Kingdom, finally fulfill the L-rd's purpose for choosing the Jewish people— to be a light to the nations. In other words, it will be in the Millennium that Israel will assume her role to teach and administer the Word of G-d to the world. The law of this Kingdom will be the Torah. When G-d gave the Torah to Israel, it was not so that Israel alone would obey it, rather Israel's obedience was to enlighten the Gentiles concerning the truths of G-d and they would understand that obeying the instructions of the L-rd leads to life and blessings, while violating these instructions brings about death and curses. Whereas originally this adherence to the Torah was not mandatory for Gentiles, but would be the result of a Gentile coming to faith in the One True G-d; in the Millennial Kingdom it will be mandated and enforced by Messiah's rule. It is for this reason the Scripture informs the reader that when Messiah returns to establish His Kingdom, He will rule with a rod of iron.

Many believers have incorrectly understood Paul's teaching to imply that faith and the Torah are incompatible. Paul never said or implied such a thing. **What he did state is that one is not**

redeemed by the works of the Law, but only by means of faith, in the all-sufficient work of Messiah Yeshua upon the cross. In the Millennial Kingdom, one will demonstrate faith in Yeshua by obeying the Word of G-d. One needs to remember that only those who took part in the Rapture will have a new and perfect body in which one will not have the ability to sin. Both Israel and the nations will not have this new body and will have the capacity to sin. Sin must be handled according to the Torah and atonement must be made to avoid punishment being applied to the violator by Messiah.

Many believers often protest and assert that such sacrifices are in conflict with the message of the Gospel, which is founded on faith and not works. The Gospel is indeed founded on faith, but the Millennial Kingdom poses an interesting situation. Since Messiah's ascension into heaven, believing in Yeshua is totally an issue of faith. When Yeshua spoke to His disciple Thomas, who refused to exercise faith unless he should see the nail prints in Yeshua's hands and the place where the sword pierced Yeshua's side, Yeshua said to him,

> "*Bring your finger here, and see My hands; and bring your hand and cast into My side; and do not be faithless, rather believe.*" John 20:27

Yeshua scolded Thomas for having to see with his eyes in order to believe. Yeshua also stated those who come to faith because of seeing, are not blessed in the same manner as those who did not see, yet believed (See John 20:29). One needs to remember that in the Millennial Kingdom Yeshua will be present. He will be ruling from the Holy of Holies in Jerusalem. For one to ask another, "Do you believe in Yeshua" in one sense will be a meaningless question because every eye will see Him. The one who disobeys Him will meet His rod of iron. The question is not at all in the Millennium, "Do you believe in Yeshua", that is "Does He exist", "Is He the L-rd's Anointed"; Yeshua is there, He is the King, His rule is not a debatable matter. Rather, the question is "Are you going to obey Him"? Obedience in the Millennial Kingdom will be displayed through the framework of the Torah.

Obviously Torah law involves sacrifices, and many understand these sacrifices to be in conflict with Messiah's death on the Cross. However, this is not the case; as many evangelicals properly teach, these sacrifices do not add to Yeshua's work, as His work was absolutely sufficient. These sacrifices are offered in memorial to Yeshua's death on the cross. In order for one to appreciate this issue, he must understand the difference between atonement and redemption. Atonement only covers the sin; however, it does not remove the need for punishment. Atonement only delays the punishment. These sacrifices, which took place on the altar, always anticipated a superior sacrifice which would bring about redemption. In regard to redemption, it totally expunges the sin and removes the need for punishment altogether. Redemption is a payment which changes the status of that which is redeemed. The sacrifices in the Millennial Kingdom will be similar in one sense to the sacrifices prior to Yeshua's death, which all pointed to His redemptive work.

The deceased Lubavitcher Rebbe, Menachem Mendel Schneerson, taught a very interesting lesson concerning the Old Testament sacrifices. He stated that there is uniqueness to the Passover sacrifice. Since Passover is the festival of redemption, one should understand the Passover lamb as an offering which achieved redemption for the Children of Israel. Rabbi Schneerson said that in a special way, all the sacrifices prior to Passover pointed to the Passover offering and the redemption it provided, and all the sacrifices thereafter, pointed back to it as well. In a parallel manner, followers of Yeshua know that His death on the cross, occurring on the fourteenth day of the Hebrew month of Nissan, was not a mere coincidence, but announced the eternal redemption that the Passover lamb in Egypt only symbolized. Hence, believers know that all the sacrifices prior to Yeshua's death pointed forward to Him and those in the Millennial Kingdom will point back to the cross.

When the Millennium begins, all those residing in it will be believers. This means that in addition to those who take part in the Rapture, there will be Jews and Gentiles alike that come to faith in the second half of the seven year period. It has already been pointed out that those who share in the Rapture receive a new and glorified body. In this new body they will not procreate. However, in regard to those who come to faith after the Rapture and during the tribulation period, even though they are saved and eternally secure in Messiah, they will be able to procreate. This fact has some important implications. Even though initially all of the residents of the Millennial Kingdom will be believers, there will be people born during the thousand years. These individuals will be expected to observe the Torah as the law of the Kingdom and will learn what it means to live in a world under the righteous rule of Messiah Yeshua. But in the end, whether or not they accept Yeshua is a personal decision. It is precisely because of the necessity of those who are born during the Millennium to make a decision concerning Yeshua that the following piece of information is stated,

"And when the thousand years should be finished, Satan will be released from his prison and will go forth to deceive the nations..." Revelation 20:7-8a

Satan's release is in accordance with the purposes of G-d. It is not that he escaped or possessed the power on his own to go forth from the prison where the L-rd had him bound. The sovereignty of G-d is not undermined by the fact that He provides these individuals with a real choice. It is hard to fathom that after living in the Kingdom of the Messiah that anyone would choose not to surrender to Yeshua and His rule. Yet, as remarkable as it is, there will be those who will choose Satan instead of Yeshua. In examining all of Revelation 20:8 one reads,

"And he shall go forth to deceive the nations, those in the four corners of the earth; Gog and Magog, to assemble them for war— the number being as the sand of the sea."

According to this verse, a great number of the very individuals who saw and experienced the righteousness of Yeshua will join with Satan to make war with the saints and attack Jerusalem (See Revelation 20:9). This war will not be accompanied with a period of tribulation like the final seven years. In fact, the clear indication from the Scripture is that this war will be very anticlimactic. As the enemies move against the people of G-d and the Holy City of Jerusalem, the reader is not told of a great battle, nor is there any mention of Messiah's coming. It is most informative that one does not read in this account any of the details that were part of the end of the tribulation period. There are those who assert that the Millennial Kingdom and the Church age are one and the same, and when Messiah returns He will establish the New Jerusalem. Such a view is impossible to reconcile with the Biblical account concerning the Millennium. All the reader is told about this war is that, as the enemy attacks, fire will come down from heaven and consume those who ally themselves with Satan.

Some point out that in regard to this war the phrase "Gog and Magog" appears. Because the Scriptures state that the war of Gog and Magog is the battle of Armageddon, should not one conclude that this war, mentioned in Revelation 20:8-9, is actually the war which concludes the tribulation period? This is not a correct assumption; the purpose of the names Gog and Magog appearing in this section is not to identify this battle as taking place at the end of the Millennium with the same conflict which Ezekiel speaks of in chapters 38 and 39. John simply uses these names to inform the reader that the same outcome which the war of Gog and Magog produced will be the outcome of those who go up to Jerusalem at the end of the Millennium. John provides a clue that he is not referring to the literal Gog and Magog in this verse. The reader should notice that the phrase before Gog and Magog is mentioned is *"those in the four corners of the earth"*. The literal Gog was the leader of the land of Magog, which most scholars identify as being North of Israel. Hence, it makes no sense to speak of the four corners of the earth with Gog and Magog, if one is using these names in a literal manner.

There are other reasons provided in this section which exegetically make it impossible to combine the Millennial Kingdom and the New Jerusalem into the same period or assert that the Millennium is actually this present age. After the defeat of those who attacked the saints and the Holy City of Jerusalem, one reads,

> "*And the Devil, the one who deceives them was cast into the lake of fire and sulfur; where the beast and the false prophet are and where they will be tortured day and night forever and ever.*" Revelation 20:10

Close attention to the Greek grammar reveals that when the Devil is released from his prison, the beast and the false prophet were not. This means that during the battle after the Millennium, the beast and false prophet were bound in the lake of fire and sulfur. It was Satan who acted alone in deceiving the nations and leading them into this battle. However, in the war of Armageddon, it is clearly stated that the beast and the false prophet were present and played a major role.

Another fact which underscores the position that the Millennial Kingdom and the New Jerusalem are not the same is the very different description one finds for Jerusalem in the Millennium and for the Eternal New Jerusalem. Special attention to this point will be given in the following chapter; let it suffice to say for now that the New Jerusalem is described using language very similar to the Garden of Eden, while such imagery is not used for the Millennial Jerusalem.

Isaiah's View of the Millennium

An entire book could be written about the information which Isaiah provides concerning the Millennium. The purpose of this section is to present a brief summary of the final two chapters of Isaiah's prophecy and demonstrate that the events which the Prophet describes could only take place in the Millennial Kingdom and not the New Jerusalem. The first part of chapter 65 is the L-rd's response to Israel's prayer in the previous chapter. In this prayer, there are clear references to the fact that the Land of Israel, including Jerusalem, is in ruin and the Jewish people are suffering greatly. In His response to this prayer, G-d states emphatically that their suffering and the physical condition of the land is all because of Israel's rebellion,

> "*I have stretched forth My hands all day to a highly disobedient people, who walk in a way which is not good, after their own thoughts.*" Isaiah 65:2

The Hebrew word which I translated "highly disobedient" also appears in Deuteronomy 21:18. It speaks of a son who is so rebellious and disobedient that his parents will take him to the judges of the city in order for him to be stoned to death by the men of the city. Therefore, Isaiah is underscoring that the spiritual condition of the Jewish people is indeed the cause for her very difficult physical condition. In spite of Israel's idolatry and numerous other sins, G-d will not utterly destroy her; in fact, He will move and return the Jewish people to their land and the places which were desolate will blossom (See Isaiah 65:8-10). Even though Israel will be reestablished, her suffering is not over because once returned to the land, she will continue to act inappropriately and a time of harsh punishment will befall her. However, this time Israel's suffering will bring about a significant change in the people. They will finally respond to the L-rd according to the truth,

> "*The one who blesses himself in the land will bless himself in the G-d of Amen, and the one who takes an oath in the land will swear in the G-d of Amen; for the previous troubles will be forgotten, for they are hidden from My eyes.*" Isaiah 65:16

It is most interesting how G-d is referred to in this verse, "*The G-d of Amen*". The Hebrew word "amen" relates to two important concepts— faith and truth. It is because Israel will finally respond to the L-rd according to the truth and with faith, that G-d will manifest His faithfulness to her and fulfill the promises He made in His word. One should not assume that it is man's faithfulness which causes G-d to be faithful. It is clear here, and in every other place where it is mentioned that one repents and turns to G-d, that it is the L-rd Who initiates the response of man.

In the next verse of Isaiah, G-d reveals what His ultimate plan is:

"For behold, I am creating a new heaven and a new earth, for the former things will not be remembered and these things will (no longer) *be upon* (one's) *heart."* Isaiah 65:17

The phrase *"new heaven and a new earth"* has caused some to incorrectly associate the events of this chapter with the New Jerusalem which the book of Revelation states is the outcome of G-d creating a *"new heaven and a new earth"*. The error which must be avoided is to assume that because this phrase appears, the New Jerusalem is what is being described. What this passage teaches is that the Millennial Kingdom is a necessary part of the preparation for the New Jerusalem. One must pay close attention to the grammar which is utilized in this verse. The same word which is found in this verse is also found in Genesis 1:1.

"In the beginning G-d created the heavens and the earth..."

One should note that the verb which both passages have in common is in a different tense in the two verses. In the Genesis text the verb is in the past tense *"created"*, while in the Isaiah text the verb is in the present tense. Students of the Hebrew Bible know that the use of the present tense is somewhat rare; hence, Isaiah is emphasizing that the creation of a *"new heaven and a new earth"* is in process but not yet a reality in this chapter of Isaiah. The proof for such an interpretation is found a few verses later in this chapter.

"It shall not be from there any longer a young child or an old man who will not fulfill his days; for a youth is a hundred years old and the sinner who will die at a hundred years old will be (considered as) *cursed."* Isaiah 65:20

This verse reveals that during the Millennium people will live much longer, so that a hundred year old will be considered to be a mere youth and a sinner who has his life ended at a hundred years old will be considered to be highly cursed. This is not the situation today, and will not be the situation in the New Jerusalem either, because the Word of G-d specifically states that in the New Jerusalem there will no longer be death (See Revelation 21:4). Therefore, since Isaiah reveals a time which could not be considered today, and is not the New Jerusalem, then there must be a Millennial Kingdom, which is not the period from the Messiah's ascension to His Second coming, i.e. today, nor will it be the immediate outcome when Yeshua returns. Hence, there is a Millennial Kingdom and those who either assert it is now, or it is synonymous with the New Jerusalem, are in error.

The Great White Throne Judgment

John states that immediately after the Millennial Kingdom an event will take place prior to G-d creating the New Jerusalem. This event is normally referred to as the "Great White Throne Judgment". A key clue which assists the reader in understanding the uniqueness of this judgment, and who will be part of this judgment, is the term resurrection. The book of Revelation speaks about two resurrections. The first resurrection has an entirely different theme to that of the second resurrection. Whereas those who are part of the first resurrection are said to be blessed and holy,

> "*Blessed and holy are the ones who have a part in the first resurrection; upon these the second death has no power, they will be priests of G-d and of the Messiah and will rule with Him a thousand years.*" Revelation 20:6

Those who are in the second resurrection will find everlasting death. The first resurrection includes all believers throughout all the various ages, while the second resurrection includes all that died without faith in Messiah Yeshua throughout all the various ages. This means that all those who rejected the Gospel throughout history, including those in the Millennial Kingdom, will take part in this second resurrection. Once again, for those who assert that since Messiah's ascension the Millennium has begun, a difficult problem presents itself. Clearly the Rapture is one of the stages of the first resurrection. Because it is clear that the Rapture has not yet occurred, but that the first resurrection is complete prior to the Millennial Kingdom, one may not assert that believers are living in the Millennium today. Such an assertion is without a Scriptural foundation.

It is clear that **all** who appear before the Great White Throne will be judged according to their deeds and therefore will be found insufficient to enter the New Jerusalem. The only ones who are granted the privilege to share eternity with G-d and the Lamb are those who have had their names written in the Lamb's Book of Life. This is an outcome which is solely the result of the redemptive work of Yeshua on the cross and was bestowed freely only upon all who receive the Gospel. **All** who appear before the Great White Throne will find themselves being cast into the lake of fire and sulfur. It is this act which the Bible calls the "Second Death" (See Revelation 20:11-15).

Chapter 13

"The New Jerusalem"

The final two chapters of the book of Revelation speak about a new reality; both a physical and a spiritual reality called the New Jerusalem. As has been discussed, the Gospel is G-d's only message of redemption and the New Jerusalem is the ultimate outcome of Yeshua's work of redemption. The New Jerusalem should rightly be understood as a new creation, distinct and removed from the first creation. John emphasizes this when he defines the New Jerusalem as a "...*new heaven and a new earth for the first heaven and first earth passed away*"(Revelation 21:1). This verse also states that in the New Jerusalem there will be no sea. This of course is in contrast to the fact that during the Millennial Kingdom the sea does exist, as it is only after the Millennium that the reader is told that the sea gives up its dead (See Revelation 20:13).

When John speaks about the New Jerusalem, he refers to it as the Holy City and describes it as a bride which has been prepared for her husband. This language is most similar to how believers are described in Revelation 19:7-8, at the time of the Second Coming. What is the purpose of this similarity? This similarity affirms the special relationship and strong attachment Messiah's followers should have for Jerusalem. This is clearly demonstrated by the Psalmist,

"*If I forget you, O Jerusalem, may my right hand forget* (its skill), *may my tongue cleave to the roof of my mouth if I do not remember you; if I do not exalt you, O Jerusalem, above my chief gladness*. Psalm 137:5-6

This imagery of marriage in the New Jerusalem—between the bride and the L-rd—hints to the great intimacy that will exist in the New Jerusalem between her residents and G-d. It is this intimacy which the next verse addresses.

> "*And I heard a great voice from heaven saying, 'Behold the tabernacle of G-d is with man and He will dwell with them; and they will be His people and G-d Himself will be with them— their G-d.*" Revelation 21:3

G-d dwelling with man and sharing intimacy with him has always been G-d's desire and is foundational in understanding the purpose of redemption. Throughout the book of Revelation it is the Temple to which John refers, so why now is the term tabernacle utilized? In order to understand the reason for this, one must acquaint himself with the Biblical language. Both in Hebrew and Greek the word "tabernacle" is formed from the word which means "to dwell". This is not the case with the word for "Temple". Hence, John was inspired to refer to the tabernacle in order to emphasize G-d dwelling with man and the intimacy which will stem from this. Judaism, in wanting to emphasize the concept of redemption, uses the frequently repeated phrase in the Old Testament which John also adapts in this verse— *They will be His people and He will be their G-d.*" When John alters the verse, his change actually strengthens the message of intimacy and how personal the relationship will be which G-d will have with those who have been redeemed.

As wonderful as the Millennial Kingdom will be with Yeshua reigning and enforcing the righteousness of the Torah, the New Jerusalem will be greater. With its establishment, all the effects of sin will be removed. This is the intent of John's proclamation that there will be no more sorrow, pain, or death (Revelation 21:4). Even though many English translations use the same phrase for the first heaven and earth passing away as they do with sorrow, pain and death passing away, the Greek word is somewhat different. Although the same root is used in both texts, a different prefix appears in the two verses. The proper understanding of this is that while the first heaven and earth were no more because of a new creation, i.e. the New Jerusalem, the fact that there is no more sorrow, pain, or death is simply an outcome or byproduct of the New Jerusalem.

An important difference between the Millennium and the New Jerusalem is the rule of law. It has been stated several times that when Yeshua rules over Israel and the nations in the Millennial Kingdom, He will do so according to the Torah. This will not be the case in the New Jerusalem. In Yeshua's famous Sermon on the Mount He taught,

> *"Do not think that I have come to destroy the Torah or the Prophets; I have not come to destroy, rather to fulfill. For truly I say to you until the heavens and the earth will be made to pass away; one **iota** or one **keraia** will not be made to pass away from the Torah; until all things will be new."*
>
> Matthew 5:17-18

Although there is great significance in these two verses in regard to several issues, the primary relevance for the New Jerusalem is that Yeshua is clearly teaching that there will be a time when the Torah will no longer be applicable for man. When is this time? The Torah will cease to be the means which G-d uses to determine right and wrong only after the first heaven and earth pass away. It is significant that in regard to the verb which is translated "pass away" in this section, the reader needs to be aware that it is also the exact same verb which appears in Revelation 21:1. However, in the Matthew passage, the mood is switched from the active voice to the passive. What are the implications of this? Yeshua is stressing that this transition from the first heaven and earth to that of the second heaven and earth, i.e. the New Jerusalem, will not just happen on its own, but rather it must be brought about. Obviously such an action is reserved for the Living G-d alone.

It is not that the Torah is no longer true, for truth is eternal. When one says that the Torah is not relevant, it is because of the fact that all things in the New Jerusalem are new! In other words, the Torah, which manifested the truths of G-d and how one finds life and blessing, rather than death and curse, will no longer be applicable, because only life and blessing will be present in the New Jerusalem. Since there is absolutely no possibility of encountering death or curse, there is simply no longer a need for the Torah.

The King in the Field

It has already been emphasized that redemption brings about intimacy with G-d. When studying the book of Revelation, one finds that this intimacy changes with the different stages of the last days. If one were to divide the end times into three distinct epochs in time, he would find the level of intimacy which the Messiah has with His people varies. Prior to the giving of the Holy Spirit, an individual could be in the presence of Yeshua, but this alone does not necessarily guarantee any degree of intimacy. However, with the giving of the Holy Spirit, every believer has a personal and eternal relationship with Yeshua. It is this type of relationship with the Messiah, by means of the Holy Spirit, which represents the first type of intimacy. With the return of Yeshua, and the establishing of the Millennial Kingdom, a new type of intimacy is brought about. Not only does the first type of relationship continue, but now through His personal rule a greater knowledge of the Messiah is achieved and because of His rule, righteousness is maintained. This is the second type of intimacy. The believer just does not read about the will and justice of G-d, he experiences it firsthand.

With the creation of the New Jerusalem and the fact that the dwelling place of G-d is with man (See Revelation 21:3) the third and final type of intimacy will be experienced. In order to help one understand this perfect expression of G-d's intimacy with man, a Chassidic anecdote will be examined. In Judaism the month of Elul holds a special significance. This month is set aside for self inspection and repentance. Chassidic thought teaches that during the month of Elul G-d is available to hear man's prayers of forgiveness in a unique way and will assist him in his desire to repent. Because repentance in its most basic meaning involves turning to G-d, with the purpose of experiencing Him, Chassidic thought describes the month of Elul with the expression, "The king is in the field". The point is that as long as the king is inside his palace, the average citizen does not have any access to him, and therefore does not experience him. However, if the king should come out from behind his palace walls and be in the field, then the commoner could approach him and make his petition. Hence, the expression, "The king is in the field" teaches that the month of Elul is unique, as the king, i.e. G-d, has come forth from His palace and is available to man in a special way.

In the New Jerusalem, Yeshua will not be ruling from the Temple, for there is no Temple in the New Jerusalem (See Revelation 21:22). His dwelling place will be with men and therefore one will have perfect and eternal access and intimacy with the Living G-d. It is this aspect of intimacy that is emphasized in the New Jerusalem.

He gave the right to become sons of G-d

In one sense, from the moment a person accepts Yeshua, he becomes a child of G-d and as a child of the One True G-d there are benefits. In the section which addresses the New Jerusalem one finds the verse,

*"The one who overcomes will inherit all things, and I will be for him G-d, and he will be for Me **the** son."* Revelation 21:7

One of the reasons that I take the time to translate the verses from the original language is that most translations are not as concerned with the exact wording, rather they often compromise precision for readability. In Revelation 21:7, the Greek text emphasizes an aspect which is lost in English translations. In this verse there is a wonderful promise that G-d makes to every believer. In reviewing the various translations of the aforementioned text, most translate the verse that the believer "...will be My (G-d's) son". Greek is a very precise language and it would have been very easy for John to have written this, but he did not. Instead John wrote that every believer would be likened to **the son**! The point the verse makes is that every believer will be recognized and treated as though he is G-d's only son. This verse strongly emphasizes the personal intimacy that each believer will enjoy for eternity with G-d.

These aspects are all but lost with how translations such as the *New International Version* (NIV) render this verse. Here is the NIV's translation of the verse:

> "*Those who are victorious will inherit all this, and I will be their God and they will be my children.*"

The NIV failed in many ways when translating this verse from the Greek. First, the NIV placed the subject "the one who overcomes" in the plural instead of the singular. Second, instead of using the masculine "son" the NIV took another liberty in attempting to be more inclusive and rendered it "children". This is highly ill-advised, because it fails to recognize cultural norms which often times can offer insight to the reader. A "son" was the preferred heir. Hence when the verse has within its context the idea of inheritance, to change it to the plural and use a neuter designation (children) it fails to capture the very emphasis of the text. Finally the text does not say that the believer will be God's son using the Greek genitive; rather it uses the dative case. English readers may find this somewhat awkward, but the original audience would have found the use of the dative to be such an encouragement.

One must remember the context for the book of Revelation. John was writing from exile. The Romans were brutally persecuting Jewish individuals and believers. John addresses in this verse "the one who overcomes". In light of what believers will encounter in the last days, this verse is a call to persevere and remain faithful in spite of great suffering. It contains a wonderful promise that is not given to all believers in a general way, meaning that one should hear it as part of a large group who will be rewarded.

Quite the contrary, the Greek text makes this promise individualistic and highly personal. G-d is not making this statement to some vast number of believers; rather He makes this promise speaking to each individual believer and addresses him as though this one is His only son. It is important for the reader to pay attention to the definite article in this verse.

It will assist one in understanding this issue when comparing the NIV with a more accurate translation, The *Young's Literal Translation*. (See below the two translations, first the NIV and then Young's.)

> "*Those who are victorious will inherit all this, and I will be their God and they will be my children.*" **New International Version**

> "He who is overcoming shall inherit all things, and I will be to him – **a** God, and he shall be to me -- **the** son," *Young's Literal Translation*

Within the *Young's Literal Translation* I highlighted the articles, both the indefinite "a" and the definite "the". *Young's* translation perfectly reflects the intent of the Greek. Whereas my translation did not place the indefinite article "a" before the word "G-d" (there is no word in the Greek language for the indefinite article, in English one may reflect it with the word "a"). I chose not to include this word before "G-d", because the phrase "a G-d" in English may cause the reader to have an inaccurate view of G-d. One would expect there to be a definite article before the word "G-d". The fact that there is not one there, yet there is the definite article before "son", only serves to enhance the intimate position that the believer will have with G-d in the New Jerusalem. In fact, all the grammatical characteristics of this verse are there to reflect what this verse wanted to stress— the personal relationship which the believer will have with G-d for eternity.

The Bride and the New Jerusalem

Earlier in this chapter it was discussed that John uses the same term "bride" in relating to both the saints and the New Jerusalem. In Revelation 21:9 one of the seven angels who had the seven bowls of G-d's wrath was given the task to reveal "*the bride, the Lamb's wife*". What follows is a vision of the Holy City, including its walls, gates, foundations, and size. When examining these details, one cannot help but encounter the same number over and over. This number is 12. It has already been pointed out that the number 12 relates to the people of G-d, so it should not be surprising that in this section the reader is told that there were 12 gates in a great and high wall of the Holy City. In these gates were written the 12 names of the 12 Tribes of Israel. Next, it is revealed that the wall of the city had 12 foundations. In these 12 foundations were the names of the 12 Apostles.

It is very significant that the names of the Apostles are in the foundation, while the names of the Tribes are in the great wall. The idea revealed here is that the Apostles are supporting Israel. Obviously the Apostles represent the Church; hence true believers should support Israel! This is not to condone every action that the modern State of Israel makes, but rather to realize that G-d has not forsaken His people. The fact that so many Jewish individuals are returning to the Land of Israel is strong support of this, especially when the Prophets promised that this would happen in the last days. Unfortunately, today more and more "believers" are open to or even call for the creation of a Palestinian State. Such a position is inconsistent with G-d's plan for His Old Testament people. The dimensions of the New Jerusalem also are derived from the number 12 (See Revelation 21:16-17). Because this number relates to the people of G-d and G-d dwells in the Holy City, once again the intent of the vision is to show the unity between the residents of the New Jerusalem and the L-rd. The statement mentioned earlier, that the bride of the Lamb is the City, simply foreshadowed this idea which the dimensions underscore.

The Garden of Eden Revisited

In the final chapter of the book of Revelation, the New Jerusalem is clearly likened to the Garden of Eden. Although there are many similarities between these two places, the differences are what is most telling. While the Garden of Eden had both the Tree of the Knowledge of Good and Evil and the Tree of Life, in the New Jerusalem there will only be the Tree of Life. This is because both death and curse came from the Tree of Knowledge of Good and Evil. In the New Jerusalem, death and curse will not exist (See Revelation 21:4 and 22:3). Another important difference is that in the Garden of Eden there were four rivers, while in the New Jerusalem just one. It is most interesting that the reader is told that on both sides of the river is the Tree of Life.

Why did the Garden of Eden have four rivers and the New Jerusalem just one? As has been discussed, the number four relates to the world, while the number one relates to G-d, "*Hear O Israel the L-rd our G-d, the L-rd is ONE*" (See Deuteronomy 6:4). Other trees are mentioned in the Garden of Eden (See Genesis 2:16); but in the New Jerusalem, only the Tree of Life is noted. What is uniquely stated about the Tree of Life in the New Jerusalem is that it will produce 12 types of fruit.

"...(The) *Tree of life which makes 12 fruits, in the course of a month, each one giving its fruit; and the leaves of the Tree for the healing of the nations.*" Revelation 22:2

One of the implications of this verse is that no matter in what month a person will approach the Tree, there will be fruit. This fact may explain one of Yeshua's actions. Once Yeshua was hungry and He went to a fig tree, expecting to find figs, but He found none. The text informs the reader it was not the season for figs. In response to the lack of figs, Yeshua cursed the fig tree and on the next day when the disciples passed by the same fig tree they noticed that it had died. Why would Yeshua become angry with the fig tree's lack of figs, since it was not the time for figs? How could He have not known that it was not the season for figs?

This passage illustrates an important truth. The reader is told that there were leaves on the fig tree, meaning it was alive. Therefore, Yeshua judged the tree, but not according to the expectations of this world; that is, whether or not it was the proper season for the tree to produce figs. Rather, He judged the fig tree according to the standards of G-d which will be reflected in the New Jerusalem. This is perhaps also how the trees behaved in the Garden of Eden. In other words, according to the will of G-d, a tree was intended to produce fruit not just in a particular season, but each and every month. Therefore, because there were no figs the tree was punished.

This passage should send a strong message to each individual. All too often one evaluates himself based upon the standards of this world, instead of the standards of G-d. When one is judged, it will not be based on some inferior set of standards because of the consequence of sin. Rather, man will be judged according to the original standards which G-d had for man at creation.

The reader is also told that in the New Jerusalem the Tree of Life will have leaves which are for the healing of the nations. This statement is somewhat surprising because with the revelation that there will be no more pain or death (See Revelation 21:4), one could rightly expect that there would not be any sickness either. Scholars have wrestled with the significance of this statement since it was written. Perhaps the key piece of information in assisting one to interpret it is the statement that the leaves are for the "*healing of the nations*". Within the book of Revelation there is a distinction made between the Church and the nations. It was only the Church that took part in the Rapture and received a new and perfect body. Even though after the Rapture, a remnant of the nations and Israel came to faith, there is no clear indication that they, too, received a new body. This has caused some to conclude that, in order for there not to be any death in the New Jerusalem G-d has provided the leaves of the Tree of Life so those who did not take part in the Rapture can continue to live for all of eternity.

Our study of the New Jerusalem will conclude with the verse,

> "*And they will see His face and His Name is upon their forehead.*" Revelation 22:4

This verse teaches two important truths which those who are in the New Jerusalem will enjoy. First, citizens of the New Jerusalem will always see the face of G-d. In order to understand the meaning of this statement, one must first realize it is a Hebrew idiom. A similar statement is made by Yeshua when He informs His disciples that the angels of children always see the face of G-d (See Matthew 18:10). The basis for interpreting these two passages is found in what is called in Hebrew the "Birkat Hakohenim". This is found in the book of Numbers:

> "*The L-rd will bless you and will guard you, He will make His face shine unto you and He will be gracious to you, the L-rd will lift up His face unto you and He will set upon you peace.*"
> Numbers 6:24-26

The verse reveals that the expression "to see or find the face of G-d" means to be blessed. Hence, in the New Jerusalem all residents will find themselves experiencing the blessing of G-d for eternity. The second half of Revelation 22:4 is also related to the verse which follows the Numbers 6 passage. This involves the Name of G-d. The word "name" in the Bible is often times synonymous with the concept of character. Thus, when John writes that "*His Name is upon their forehead*", it implies that the residents of the New Jerusalem will always think, and therefore express with their actions, the character of G-d. It is not a coincidence that after the passage from Numbers 6:24-26, one reads,

> "*And they* (the Priests) *placed My Name upon the Children of Israel and I will bless them.*" Numbers 6:27

The uniting of the two ideas mentioned in Revelation 22:4 teaches that the true blessing is when one can behave in such a way that he manifests the character of G-d through his actions.

This will be the eternal reality for those who are in the New Jerusalem. This outcome reflects the primary aspect of the New Jerusalem, that one will experience perfect personal intimacy with the Living G-d.

Afterword

"Israel and the Middle East"

Even though Israel has always made the headlines in the world news, there seems to be an increasing amount of attention which this tiny country is receiving in the world press. Perhaps G-d is behind this. Scripture demands that one pay attention to Israel in the last days, so in order to assist the world, the L-rd is making sure that Israel and what is taking place there is a major topic in the media. A very important question which each person who wants to understand G-d's behavior in the end times must answer is, "How are the Jewish people and the Land of Israel connected to G-d's plan of redemption and the establishment of His Kingdom?"

Sadly, many Christians answer this question that there is nothing at all unique about the Jewish people today in regard to G-d's plan of redemption, nor is the Land of Israel connected to the establishment of His Kingdom any more than any other nation or place on the earth. For one to make such a statement, a wealth of prophecy must be ignored or set aside. Replacement theologians see Israel as a "rebel nation" for much of her history. While this is true, G-d has always moved to bring the people back into a relationship with Him in order that His purposes would be accomplished. A beautiful example of this faithfulness of G-d is found in Daniel's prayer in the ninth chapter of Daniel. At this time, the 70 years of exile had come to an end. Therefore, Daniel prayed with full assurance that G-d would bring about the means for the people to return to the Land of Israel. Replacement theologians understand G-d returning the Jewish people to the Land of Israel as necessary preparation for the Messiah's advent. However, they rule out any possibility for Israel to be returned to the land prior to the Messiah's Second Coming. It is to this point, based upon numerous prophecies; I am compelled to respectfully disagree. As mentioned in chapter three of this book, a study of a few of these key prophecies will be presented.

First, Isaiah informs his readers that the Jewish people will, in the last days, return to the land according to the commandment of the L-rd. In the following passage, Isaiah expressly states that the Jewish people must settle in the places where they dwelt previously.

"Shout O barren one who has not born, break out into a shout and in joy, who has not been in labor; for more are the children of the desolate than the married, says the L-rd. Spread out the place of your tent, let the curtains of your dwelling places stretch out, do not withhold; lengthen your cords and make strong your tent pegs. For you shall spread out right and left and your descendant shall inherit the nations; and the desolate cities they will settle. Fear not for you will not be shamed, for you will not be humiliated, for you will not be disgraced; for the shame of your youth you will forget, and the disgrace of your widowhood you will not remember any more. For your Husband is your maker—The L-rd of Hosts is His name; and your Redeemer is the Holy One of Israel; the G-d of all the earth will He be called. For as a wife is forsaken and sad, the L-rd has called you and a wife of one's youth she will be despised says your G-d. In a brief moment I have left you and in great mercy I will gather you. In a fury I concealed My face from you for a moment and in eternal grace I am merciful to you says your Redeemer—the L-rd. For like the waters of Noah, this is to Me which I have sworn, the waters of Noah will not pass over the land again, thus I have sworn not to be wrathful unto you nor to rebuke you. For the mountains may be removed and the hills may collapse, but My grace will not be removed from you and My covenant of peace will not collapse says the L-rd Who shows you mercy." Isaiah 54:2-10

Replacement theologians like to unite the first verse of this passage with Paul's quotation of it in Galatians 4:27. In this section, Paul shares the rabbinical view that the barren woman, to which the passage alludes, is Jerusalem. In Paul's inspired use of the Isaiah passage, he understands it as the heavenly Jerusalem. There is no disagreement that ultimately believers in Yeshua are the true children of G-d and the residents of the New Jerusalem. **The point of contention is whether Paul is stating categorically that this prophecy only has a fulfillment through believers in Yeshua dwelling in the New Jerusalem or could Paul solely be utilizing the first verse of the Isaiah passage because of the great gladness and joy which is expressed in this verse. Perhaps Paul removed this verse from the passage it belongs to for the purpose of expressing the great joy and happiness which he wanted to emphasize in regard to the subject he was sharing with the Galatians.** The fact that Paul states emphatically in the Galatians passage, when speaking about Sarah and Hagar, that he is allegorizing them should be a sufficient indication. In other words, even though Paul likens Hagar to the current Jerusalem which was in bondage and Sarah to the New Jerusalem, this in no way whatsoever denies the reality of the historical situation that Hagar and Sarah literally experienced. Paul actually lifts the verse from Isaiah 54 from its context, Israel's future return from exile to the land which G-d promised her, in order to heighten the reader's understanding of the ultimate future fulfillment of the Abrahamic Covenant. The question that Replacement theologians must answer is, "Is it proper hermeneutical methodology to ignore or even deny the reality of the prophecy from which the verse was taken?" Paul's context in Galatians chapter four was not whether or not G-d would return the Jewish people once again to the Land of Israel. Rather he was speaking about the Mosaic Law in light of a proper understanding of the Abrahamic Covenant. Hence, to offer Galatians 4:27 as New Testament proof which supports Israel's loss of the right to resettle, in the last days, in the land which G-d promised them is exegetically invalid.

Had Replacement theologians examined in greater detail the entire prophecy, they would see that the context rules out applying this prophecy to believers. For Isaiah states,

"In a brief moment I have left you and in great mercy I will gather you. In a fury I concealed My face from you for a moment and in eternal grace I am merciful to you says your Redeemer—the L-rd." Isaiah 54:7-8

These verses could only apply to natural descendants of Jacob and never to the Church. For when has G-d, Who has promised believers, "*I will never leave you or forsake you*" and "*Behold I am with you always*" (See Hebrew 13:5 and Matthew 28:20) ever left us? When has He ever concealed His face from us?

The best interpreter of the Scripture is the Scriptures. Hence, the fact that there are numerous other passages which support that the L-rd will return the Jewish people to the Land of Israel prior to the establishment of the Kingdom, should have demonstrated to Replacement theologians that such an assertion concerning Isaiah 54 was errant. This passage confirms not only G-d's plan to have the Jewish people resettle the land, but also the fact that even though Israel will suffer greatly for her disobedience, the covenant will be maintained by G-d Himself and not be fulfilled by different means.

Not only does Isaiah speak about the Jewish people's return to the Land of Israel in the last days, but so does the Prophet Jeremiah.

"Woe, O shepherds who scatter and spread the flock of My pasture, says the L-rd. Therefore, thus says the L-rd, the G-d of Israel, concerning the shepherds who shepherd My people, you scattered My flock and drove them away and will I not visit upon them; behold I will visit upon you the wickedness of your deeds, says the L-rd. I will gather up the remnant of My flock from all the lands which I have dispersed them there, I will return them to their pleasant places and they shall be fruitful and multiply. I will establish for them shepherds and they shall shepherd them and they shall no longer be afraid nor dismayed and they shall not be visited (by their enemies) says the L-rd. Behold the days are coming says the L-rd, and I

will establish for David the Righteous Branch and a King will reign and be prosperous; He will execute justice and righteousness in the land. In those days, Judah and Israel will be saved; they will dwell in security and this is His name which He shall be called, the L-rd our Righteousness. Therefore behold, the days are coming says the L-rd, when they will no longer say, 'As the L-rd lives Who brought up the children of Israel from the land of Egypt; but rather, As the L-rd lives, Who brought up and brought back the seed of the house of Israel from the land of the North and from all the countries where I scattered them there and they shall dwell on their own land.'" Jeremiah 23:1-8

This prophecy from Jeremiah is very specific and it is the details of this passage which prohibit one from forming a theology which asserts that the Church replaces Israel and all which was promised to Israel is fulfilled by believers. The first thing which must be pointed out about this prophecy is that it is Messianic; that is, it speaks to the end of this age. It is very significant that in the middle of this section David is mentioned. This is not a reference to King David, who lived 3,000 years ago, but the Son of David, Messiah Yeshua. This fact is confirmed by the additional statement that this One is also known as the "Righteous Branch". This One is called a King who will reign, i.e. in the future.

Another key piece of information is that this prophecy foretells of an exodus for the Jewish people. Whereas the first great exodus was out of the land of Egypt, the final great exodus will be from two destinations. The text emphasizes first *"the North"* and then *"from all the countries where I scattered them"*. It concludes with the promise that the Jewish people *"will dwell on their own land."* This passage is understood by every rabbi who holds to some level of authority for the Bible, to pertain to the Jewish people, and that its fulfillment will be in the time shortly before the Messiah will establish His Kingdom. This prophecy is so clear that the men of the Great Assembly wrote in the Shemoneh Ezreh (the foundational prayer for every Jewish worship service) the following blessing:

"May the Righteous Branch of David Your servant quickly spring forth and His triumph be lifted up in Your salvation; for Your salvation we have hoped every day. Blessed are You O L-rd, Who causes the triumph of salvation to spring forth."

I realize many Christians could care less how rabbis may interpret a passage, but an objective person who looks at all the Scriptural indicators present in this passage, must agree upon a few conclusions, not just by a consensus, but unanimously. First, the exodus to which this passage alludes has not happened previously. It is either in the future or currently taking place. Perhaps the more than one million Jewish people, who have left the former Soviet Union (North of Israel) and immigrated to Israel over the last thirty years, should cause one to ponder the precision of Jeremiah's words. Second, the numerous Jews who have immigrated to Israel, since its formation, are from a wide variety of other countries. Third, this prophecy is connected to the end times and the establishment of the Kingdom of the Messiah. Fourth, the context is clear, only the Jewish people could possibly be the subject of this prophecy and not believers, as believers were never brought up from the land of Egypt.

The prophet Ezekiel makes this same point concerning the Jewish people's return to the Land of Israel, and likewise links this to the Messiah.

"And say unto them, 'Thus says the L-rd G-d, behold, I am taking the children of Israel from among the nations, where they have gone, and I will gather them from all around and I will bring them to their own land. I will make them one nation in the land, in the mountains of Israel, and one King shall be for them for a king and they shall no longer be two nations, nor shall they be divided into two kingdoms any longer. And they shall not be contaminated any longer with their idols, or with their abominations, or in their transgressions; but I will save them from all their dwelling places which they have sinned in them. I will purify them and they shall be for Me for a people. And I will be for them

(their) G-d. And My Servant David will be a King over them and one Shepherd shall be over them and in My judgments they shall walk and My laws they shall keep. And they shall do them. And they shall dwell upon the land which I gave to My servant Jacob, in which their fathers dwelt, and they shall dwell upon it, they and their sons and their sons' sons forever, and David My Servant, shall be Prince over them forever. And I will establish for them a covenant of peace, an eternal covenant will be with them and I shall set them and increase them and place My sanctuary in their midst forever. My dwelling place shall be among them and I will be for them (their) G-d and they shall be for Me a people, and the nations shall know that I am the L-rd that sanctifies Israel when My sanctuary is in their midst.'" Ezekiel 37:21-28

This is perhaps one of the strongest sections in the Bible which speaks to how G-d will gather up the Jewish people, not because of any merit on their part ("*And they shall not be contaminated any longer with their idols, or with their abominations, or in their transgressions*"), but because of the L-rd's grace and His faithfulness to His covenant. It is very significant that in this passage those to whom G-d is bringing to Israel are not yet believers. On the contrary, it is for the purpose of bringing them to faith that the L-rd returns the Jewish people to the Land of Israel. Another interesting aspect of this prophecy is that when Israel finally responds in faith to G-d's grace and fidelity, the nations will take notice of this and also turn to the G-d of Israel in similar faith (See Ezekiel 37:28).

As one would imagine, Replacement theologians usually ignore such prophecies altogether. However, when forced to respond to them, they allegorize and spiritualize them, failing to evaluate much of the content of these prophecies and missing out on a great example of G-d's faithfulness and failing to understand His plan to bring a greater number of people to the Gospel of Messiah Yeshua.

Faith in Messiah Forbids Support for a Palestinian State

One should not confuse opposition to a Palestinian State with a lack of concern for those individuals who live in Judea, Samaria, and Gaza who are of Arab descent. In this final section of this book, having already studied a Biblical basis for the formulation of one's view, now a brief look at some of the non-Biblical factors which one should take into consideration when determining whether one should support the establishment of a Palestinian State or not will be discussed. One of the first things that a person needs to remember is that when the modern State of Israel was established in 1948 there were already Jewish individuals living in the land that would comprise the State of Israel from 1948-1967. If one looks at the ratio between the Jewish-Arab populations in 1948 for the area that made up the pre-1967 borders, there were three Arabs for every Jew. The best estimates recorded a Jewish population of nearly 700,000.

Beginning in the 19th century, Zionism began as a desire of the Jewish people to return to their ancient homeland. Although nearly 1900 years had passed since the destruction of the Second Temple to the proclamation of the modern State of Israel in 1948, it is important to note that although other nations/empires included this land under their rule, the last government which called Israel its homeland was a Jewish one.

When the modern State of Israel was proclaimed in 1948, the response of Israel's neighbors, by and large, was to attack and make war. Jewish people who were living in this land felt a need to state formally what was happening in practice. The land along the Mediterranean coast, where these 700,000 Jews were living and where the vast majority of the Jewish people were returning to, became a primary destination for those Jews who were displaced from Europe due to the Holocaust. Even since the end of World War I, when earlier refugees were coming to this land, it became clear that some agreement had to be reached on Jewish settling in their ancient homeland. Therefore, the League of Nations was required to redraw borders in the Middle East.

Eventually the outcome was the creation of a British Mandate for Palestine. Most of the land that the British Mandate for Palestine addressed was east of the Jordan River and was not available for Jewish immigration. Hence, in the very location which had been available for Jewish immigration, a Jewish State was proclaimed.

Two years prior to this proclamation of a Modern State of Israel, the mandate for Transjordan ended, and on May 25, 1946, the modern nation of Jordan was established. The creation of the State of Israel did not uproot Palestinians. Arabs who were living in the new State of Israel were only displaced by choice. It was the fact they were defeated when they attacked Israel after the British departed, that many of the Arab inhabitants of Israel chose to abandon the land. It was because they feared retribution for their conduct that they left. An additional reason for their departure was that they were advised to because they were told by Arab leaders from other States of an impending attack that would soon follow upon the State of Israel by these surrounding Arab nations. Hence, the formation of Israel had virtually nothing to do with those who are called "Palestinian" today being displaced from the land.

An issue that often adds to the confusion of the Israeli-Palestinian conflict is a failure to make a distinction between the "Palestinian people" and Arab individuals in general. Often times people link these two different people groups together as one, failing to realize the important differences between them in regard to this conflict. The vast majority of those who are called Palestinian today lived in the State of Jordan from its creation until 1967. An accurate historical understanding of these individuals is necessary in order to form a proper view of the legitimacy of a Palestinian state.

Who are the Palestinians?

If one were asked to identify the "Palestinians", the vast majority of individuals would site those people who Yasser Arafat represented, and now who are represented by Abu Mazen and the terrorist organization Hamas. They would identity those who live west of the Jordan River in the land which Israel occupies. Most individuals fail to realize that prior to the establishment of the State of Israel in 1948; the "Palestinians" were Jewish individuals who lived in the Middle East. What is today the Jerusalem Post was called the Palestinian Post. Today's Jerusalem Symphony was then called the Palestinian Symphony, and it was comprised of Jewish individuals. The point that is being made is that prior to 1948 Jewish people were known as Palestinians, and not the ones who bear this label today. How did this change come about?

The term "Palestine" was a designation for land which once was known as "Phoenicia". This word refers to the land along the Mediterranean coast north of Egypt in what the Bible called "Canaan". The etymology of the word relates to the people in the Bible called the Philistines. Surely all will remember that the Philistines were enemies of the Children of Israel and were committed to thwarting the purposes of G-d. King David defeated the Philistines and united the Jewish people into a Kingdom with the name Israel. Prior to the establishment of ancient Israel, never was there a nation in this area of land; rather numerous ethnic groups inhabited the region in small kingdoms know as city-states.

There is evidence that the Roman Empire preferred to refer to the region by a term which was similar to the modern word Palestine. This was to underscore to the Jewish people that their nation was no more. Although modern scholarship attests that the use of the term "Palestine" by the Romans was only during the latter period of its rule, this claim seems to be in conflict with the feelings of the disciples, who asked Yeshua,

"Therefore, when they came together they were asking Him, 'L-rd, are You at this time restoring the Kingdom to Israel?'"

Acts 1:6

When exactly the Romans used the term "Palestine" is not the primary concern. Rather the point I want to communicate is that the term Palestine was historically used by the enemies of the Jewish people, and that Yeshua's disciples clearly referred to the land with the name Israel. Why so many Christians use the term Palestine in referring to what the Scripture calls Israel is quite puzzling.

It was Yasser Arafat, with help from a Madison Avenue marketing firm, who concluded that after the formation of the State of Israel, if those Arab individuals who lived in Judea, Samaria, and Gaza would apply the term to themselves, it would bolster their claim for receiving their own state. One needs to remember that these people lived in Jordan from 1946 to 1967. This being the case, why would not Mr. Arafat and his people pursue the land, which Israel captured and administered after the Six day war, to be returned to Jordan, rather than the creation of a new state altogether? There are two primary reasons for this. First, Arafat and his people did not integrate well into the new Jordanian state. There were numerous violent conflicts between these individuals and the Jordanian leadership. Such conflicts brought about the death of tens of thousands of these people. The second reason is rooted in the same issue, namely Jordan preferred to have Israel deal with these people. In fact, the late King Hussein of Jordan, in commenting about his decision to attack Israel in 1967, related the situation that he found himself in and the rationale he used in coming to the decision to attack Israel. King Hussein was motivated by several considerations; first, in order to demonstrate loyalty to his fellow Arabs; second, to be a participant on the victorious side. King Hussein believed strongly that Israel could not defeat Egypt and Syria; therefore, joining the war would place him and Jordan on the side of victory, rather than being neutral which would be viewed in the Arab world as supporting Israel. Third, he reasoned that Israel would not cross the Jordan River and even in the most unlikely event of an Israeli victory, the land he would forfeit, would in fact pass his "Palestinian problem" from Jordan to Israel. Hence it was not the formation of the State of Israel that created the Israeli-Palestinian conflict, but Israel's victory in the Six Day War and the fact that Israel administered Judea, Samaria, and Gaza (captured from Egypt). Therefore, when Israel proclaimed her independence and declared Statehood when the British Army left in 1948, it was not the crisis that frequently the world would have one to believe for the "Palestinian people". It should be pointed out that Lebanon did remain neutral during the Six Day War, because of the political instability within Lebanon and a general weakness of the country prohibited the nation from joining in the war.

Many people erroneously believe that the Israeli government is hostile to Arabs in general, persecuting them and denying them human rights. It is vital to recognize that those Arabs, who did not leave the State of Israel at the War of Independence, but chose to reside under a Jewish government, received full citizenship with all the rights and privileges pertaining to it. In fact, it is in Israel where Arabs enjoy the greatest freedoms and have the highest educational standards of anywhere in the Middle East or Asia.

For the next 19 years, Israel did not expand its border based upon the pretense of a divine right to the land or under some fictitious policy of land acquisition. Its residents lived peacefully side by side with their Arab neighbors (with the exception of the Sinai Campaign in 1956). It was only upon Arab aggression that Israel launched a pre-emptive strike in 1967. The facts are clear that the Six Day War was not an Israeli aggression to expand its land, but rather a necessary action of defense and a desire to secure her borders to ones which could be defended against further Arab aggression. Such a decision proved to be wise when, once again, Israel was faced with Arab armies mobilizing at her borders in 1973 which led to the Yom Kippur War. Israel has faced several attempts to massacre her people and destroy the nation. Defensible borders are a prerequisite for Israel's survival. Returning to the pre-1967 borders and establishing a Palestinian State in Judea, Samaria, and Gaza is not a formula for peace, but a recipe for a war which Israel would not survive without divine intervention.

As a result of the Six Day War, Israel took control of all of Jerusalem, Judea and Samaria, land that was previously part of Jordan. Due to the loss of the war, many of the Arab inhabitants of this land fled while others who remained continued to be hostile toward the Israeli government and Jewish people. Israel also took control of the Sinai (later given away to Egypt in a peace deal) and Gaza from Egypt. It is primarily today East Jerusalem, Judea and Samaria and Gaza which are at the heart of the Israeli-Palestinian conflict.

The need for a modern State of Israel became clear to most people at the end of World War II, when the world learned of the unthinkable reality of the Holocaust (See UN General Assembly Resolution 181, November 29, 1947). Israel has demonstrated a sincere desire not to rule over the Palestinian people, granting them autonomy and in 2000, Israel's then-Prime Minister Ehud Barak, offered the Palestinian Authority nearly all the land that Jordan possessed before attacking Israel in 1967. The exceptions to this had to do with the large Jewish communities in Judea and Samaria (including parts of Jerusalem), highway 90 in the Jordan valley and a small area on the Temple Mount for Jewish prayers. Certainly most people would see this as a reasonable settlement. What did then Prime Minister Barak want for these concessions? PM Barak demanded just one thing, a promise to an end of violence against Israelis. It is significant that the then-head of the PA, Yasser Arafat, refused this offer.

In a speech to the U.S. Congress in May of 2011, current Israeli Prime Minister Binyamin Netanyahu presented an even more generous offer which included land swaps in exchange for large Jewish settlements. In this offer Gaza was also included in the creation of a Palestinian state. This offer, in my opinion, represents the best offer the State of Israel will ever make to the Palestinian people. I am personally against any and all offers of a Palestinian state, believing it is against G-d's Word and will severely lessen Israel's security. Putting such views aside for the moment, it is most significant that the response of the Palestinian leadership was that such an offer was a declaration of war. Would an objective person believe that there exists a true peace partner with which Israel can negotiate?

In returning to Yasser Arafat's refusal of then PM Barak's offer, and the fact that the United States agreed with Israel that Arafat was not a reasonable partner, what was the Palestinian response? Over the next three years the worst uprising occurred as Palestinian terrorism soared. As hundreds of Israeli citizens met their death through bus bombings and other acts of terrorism, the world kept on insisting that Israel would show restraint. Many Christians want Israel to create a Palestinian state in a gesture of mercy based on the standards of "Biblical justice". How is it merciful to provide a state to those who are one's professed enemies, who have in their charter the expressed desire to destroy Israel? Why would Israel even entertain the idea of a Palestinian state west of the Jordan River? Those who would even suggest a Palestinian state have not only set aside the message of the Prophets, but they either ignore historical events or are ignorant of them.

Here are a few of the facts: The Palestinian people were also a problem for the Jordanian government. After losing the war with Israel, Jordan was very happy to pass this problem on to Israel. Although one should not minimize the suffering of the Palestinians, it is most significant that Israel has contributed more money and assistance to them than the Arab world in general. In actuality, the Arab world simply uses the suffering of the Palestinian people as a way to condemn the nation and the people of Israel. But what is the cause of their suffering and who is to blame?

The first point that I would like to offer is that Israelis have no desire to rule or inflict any suffering upon any people, including the Palestinians. Prior to the Six Day War in 1967, were there Jewish individuals committing acts of terror against those who resided in Judea and Samaria? The answer is no. The facts are clear that Israel was most content with her borders and left the residents of Judea and Samaria to the Jordanians. However, after the Six Day War, the residents of Judea and Samaria became by default Israel's problem. Some have suggested that Israel should have simply returned the land to Jordan with the people. Such a decision was in conflict with what many experts felt Israel needed in order to secure her people:

"On June 29, 1967, General Earl Wheeler, Chairman of the joint Chiefs-of-Staff, submitted to President Johnson a document on 'The Minimum Requirements for Israel's Defense.' According to Wheeler, the historical, geographic, topographic, political and military reality of the Middle East behooves Israel to control the mountain ridges of Judea, Samaria and the Golan Heights. In fact, the dramatic technological upgrading of Arab military forces, since 1967, has made surprise offensives (e.g. 1973, Yom Kippur War) swifter, ballistic missiles significantly more destructive and precise, population centers and IDF bases more vulnerable and the deployment of reservists (75% of Israel's military force!) much slower and problematic. Hence, there is a dramatically increasing importance of the mountain ridges of Judea and Samaria in blocking and delaying a surprise invasion, providing Israel's reservists with more time for deployment. (Without reservists, Israel would be lethally inferior to invading Arab forces).

"One hundred US retired Generals and Admirals signed a public advertisement in October 1988, contending that Israel should not withdraw from Judea and Samaria — which could not be demilitarized effectively - lest it fails to provide security to its people. The late Admiral 'Bud' Nance defined Judea and Samaria's eastern mountain ridge (3,000 foot steep slope), dominating the Jordan Valley, as 'the most effective tank barrier' and the western mountain ridge (2,000 foot moderate slope), over-towering Jerusalem and Tel Aviv, as "a dream platform for invasion to the narrow coastal plain."

This quotation was taken from an article by Yoram Ettinger in his July- August 2009 article entitled "Judea and Samaria— A Wake Up Call"

Israel has tried to live peacefully with her neighbors since 1948, but due to the expressed desire and unsuccessful intentions of her neighbors to destroy her, Israel has acquired the land that most military experts see as necessary for Israel's survival. I fear that when individuals say that Israel should seek a peaceful settlement, what they are implying is that Israel should make concessions of land. Israel has demonstrated a willingness to make unwise concessions which have brought about the deaths of more than a thousand Israelis since the infamous handshake between Yitzhak Rabin and Yasser Arafat. Not only have Israelis suffered, but so too have the Palestinians. It is most clear that since the Palestinian Authority has taken over the day to day administration of much of Judea and Samaria, and Hamas in the Gaza strip, corruption has run rampant and the social and economic situation of the residents of these places have deteriorated greatly. Some would like to blame the Israelis for this, but as more money is pumped into these places, less and less goes to the residents and more and more is put into the foreign bank accounts of its "leaders". The World Bank could not receive an accounting of the 75 million dollars it contributed to the Palestinian Authority nor does any other government or relief agency receive accountings for money given.

If Israel is guilty, she is guilty of allowing international pressure to cause her to cease to administer these places. Israel is guilty of allowing world pressure, calling her military an occupying force, to influence her from pulling out of most of Judea, Samaria, and Gaza. Let us consider Bethlehem and Gaza as examples. Many Christians have joined the international voice demanding that Israel leave Judea, Samaria, and Gaza (Israel departed from Gaza in 2006). As Israel has departed, it is very important to understand what has happened to Arab Christians in these places. They have suffered persecution from their Muslim neighbors. The PA and Hamas are Muslim organizations which want to stamp out any other religious expression. I have spoken personally to Arab Christians in these areas and can attest to the lack of human rights that are now afforded to Arab Christians because of Israel's departure. In Bethlehem, Muslim militants used a Christian neighborhood to fire at a Jewish neighborhood in Jerusalem called Gilo. Naturally Israel could not tolerate this assault on its citizens and returned fire. What occurred? The outcome was the destruction of this Arab Christian neighborhood. What does the world hear? Nothing about the cause of Israel's actions, just how the "evil occupier" destroyed the homes of "persecuted" Arabs. I believe that it is these misrepresentations of truth by the media that play a large role in people being misinformed.

What should one expect to happen in the Middle East?

There is no doubt that a military buildup is taking place in some key areas in the Middle East. Hezbollah on the North, Hamas in the Southwest, and not to mention other nations in the area, like Egypt, Turkey, Syria, and Iran, are all posing an ever increasing threat to Israel. These nations and groups are becoming more Islamic. They believe it is a Muslim's responsibility to redeem the Land of Israel for Allah. Many falsely assert that Muslims also see the Land of Israel as part of their "Holy Land" as well. This is not true, as neither Jerusalem nor any other part of the State of Israel is mentioned in the Koran. Muslims claim Israel as their land because twice Muslims ruled over Israel and, according to Islamic law, if land has ever been under Muslim ownership; it is incumbent upon Muslims to redeem this land.

It is amazing to me that those who are suppose to be people of faith, cannot see the spiritual warfare taking place. What is the region heading for? The answer is war. The initial conflict will either be the basis for the world compelling Israel to establish a Palestinian state or will come as a result of a Palestinian state having been established. This means that there will continue to be more and more international pressure placed upon Israel until finally the world community will demand, perhaps by means of sanctions, that Israel must agree to a Palestinian state.

At the time of this writing, 24 Palestinian activists (according to Syrian authorities) were killed attempting to cross the border into Israel. This "demonstration" is a classic example of Palestinian leaders, with support of the Syrian government, exploiting young men for the expressed purpose of capturing media attention.

There was absolutely no purpose in bussing young men to the Israel-Syria border and having them attempt to cross the border other than to place Israel's military in a no win situation. First of all, such an event could not have even taken place without the Syrian government's participation. The international media was quick to criticize Israel without understanding the reality of the situation. A good example of how the media misrepresents the situation is how Fox News reporter, Reena Ninan, represented the event. This "demonstration" took place on the anniversary of the Six Day War. Arabs throughout the world lament this day, because it reminds them of their defeat and Israel taking control of Judea and Samaria. However, Ms. Ninan simply reported that the day marks Israel's occupation of "Palestinian land". She did not mentioned that Egypt, Jordan, and Syria attacked Israel unprovoked. Therefore the numerous people who heard her report were left with the impression that Israel one day simply marched into land that was Palestinian and began to oppress the people. Such biased misrepresentations are standard throughout the media.

In regard to the deaths which occurred in these border "demonstrations", naturally they are unfortunate. Yet, if Israel manually captures those who cross the Israeli border and merely returns them as many in the media suggested, then the number of individuals who will attempt this will soar, as also the number of places on the border where these activities will take place. The end result is that the Israeli military will become consumed with dealing with these border demonstrations. Israel made it very clear to these demonstrators that the military would not tolerate these attempts to cross illegally into Israel. The neighboring nations were advised as well as those who assembled on the border. If protesters knew that Israel was serious (a similar demonstration on the day which marks the anniversary of Israel's independence ended the same way) and would not tolerate anyone to cross the border and those who did so would be either injured or killed, then why would Syria allow the leaders of these "demonstrations" bus people to their death? The answer is simply to bring international pressure upon the nation of Israel.

Whether by means of this international pressure or through armed conflict, the Prophet Joel reveals that Israel will be divided in the last days. One cannot be dogmatic that a Palestinian state is the fulfillment of Joel's prophecy (See Joel 4:2; 3:2 English), but combined with Obadiah's prophecy concerning a war between Israel and Edom prior to the establishment of the Kingdom of G-d, there seems to be Scriptural evidence for supporting such a view. If a Palestinian state is indeed established by an armed conflict, this will not be the major war to which Ezekiel, Zechariah, or John (Revelation) referred. This war will only come about after a Palestinian state is established.

It is important for people to understand that the arms buildup taking place in Gaza and Southern Lebanon, as well as throughout the Muslim world, be seen as a foretaste of what will occur when a Palestinian state is established. Even though Israel may demand as a condition for a Palestinian state that it be demilitarized, the reality of the situation will be exactly like what happened in Southern Lebanon after the Second Lebanese War. Israel agreed to the ceasefire that the world was demanding based upon the assurance that Southern Lebanon, below the Litani River, would be demilitarized. UNIFIL was to greatly increase the number of its personnel in order to assist in the full implementing of the Taif Accords and several UN resolutions which the ceasefire was based upon. These Accords date back to October 22, 1989, and called for a Syrian withdrawal from its influence and presence in Southern Lebanon. The fact that Hezbollah represents a Syrian influence is not a debated subject. UN resolution 1559 demanded the Lebanese government to exert its sovereignty throughout all of its country. This meant to reign in Hezbollah and to have it and all other militias to disband and declare support for the democratic process.

Israel signed this agreement and has kept her part of it. This is not the case with Lebanon. Lebanon has totally failed to carry out its obligations, as now Hezbollah is a major player in the Lebanese government. So much for an end to Syrian influence in Lebanon! Hezbollah is not only armed, but has greatly surpassed the dangerously high arsenals it possessed prior to the Second Lebanese War. In addition, an arms embargo which Israel implemented during the conflict was promised to be maintained by a multinational force. Israel agreed and removed her ships from Lebanese waters. Although a multinational force did begin to enforce the embargo, it ceased to continue after a few days, citing that cargo ships did not want to comply. Israel's objections to the UN were not responded to by the UN Security Council.

The point that cannot be stressed too much is that Israel cannot depend upon her Muslim neighbors to keep the agreements they make nor can Israel trust the international community to enforce these agreements. Israel must realize that the world is turning against the Jewish people, which will also mean turning against the Jewish state. This should not come as a surprise to any student of Bible prophecy, but the Jewish people by and large and especially Israel's leaders fail to grasp this point. G-d does not want His people to trust in alliances with nations or depend upon man for their security. Rather the L-rd G-d of Israel demands the Jew first and also the Gentile to look to Him and His Messiah, Yeshua, not just for earthly security, but eternal security.

What is taking place in the world today, and especially in the Middle East, is nothing more than G-d setting the stage for the events of prophecy to be played out. It is the humble and wise man, who will take to heart these words,

"Trust in the L-rd with all your heart, upon your own understanding, do not rely. In all your ways acknowledge Him...." Proverbs 3:5-6a

The question which you must answer is whether the Scriptures will indeed be your basis for your opinions and actions or whether you will allow the influence of the beast to lead you with him to everlasting destruction. My prayer is that you will take to heart the message of Yeshua and receive His Gospel and find your place in His Kingdom, both now and forever.

Made in the USA
Middletown, DE
25 April 2023